Lender Created Debt

Lender Created Debt

HOW INTEREST ON MONEY AFFECTS
THE HUMAN CONDITION

R D Dulin

2008

Lender Created Debt

Contents

Preface

In this discourse I have endeavored to document and explain my theory concerning a major fault in the operation of civilized society. This fault manifests itself in the inaccurate valuation and exchange of property.

The building blocks of this theory have all been stated at least in part many times in the past. I am indebted to many people's ideas, observations and years of study, both professional and amateur in defining the nature of this fault. My part is simply fitting these ideas together in a logical and defendable package.

This culmination is not a consensus of opinion or as of yet scientifically proven. With help, all of that will come in time. It is therefore at this point, my personal opinion. November 11, 2008

Introduction

L ender Created Debt" is the practice of lending money at interest and not spending all of the interest collected. The interest is hoarded repeatedly until the lender effectively owns the supply of money in a given society. It is an ancient but poorly understood practice that affects every person on the earth that is civilized enough to trade with money.

The fundamental concept and operation of "Lender Created Debt" or "LCD" will be illustrated with several simple examples. After the mechanism of LCD operation is understood, the reader will be able to follow the path that leads to specific symptoms and subsequent outcomes such as, inefficient production, antisocial behaviors, transactional exclusion and adaptive mutations in the institutions of society. These outcomes are so diverse and apparently unconnected that the suggestion that they have a common cause seems to defy logic.

Finally we will explore methods of coping with LCD. This can not be attempted with any hope of success without a working understanding of the deceptively simple mechanisms employed in the initiation and maintenance of debt. The reader is cautioned that LCD is a finely tuned operation that has evolved over several thousand years. Its evolution is not complete, and its weaknesses will become quite apparent later in this discourse. This ongoing evolutionary process includes promoting the selection of people who cannot perceive the mechanism and are tolerant of the lenders. What this means is that the reader is predisposed to dismiss thoughts and discussion concerning the mechanism of this subject and therefore might not be able to comprehend how LCD works without extraordinarily careful study. For this reason the reader is urged to study and consider carefully, the simplified scenarios that illustrate certain aspects of "Lender Created Debt" operation even though they are somewhat tedious. The genius of Lender Created Debt is that it is so simple that it is unbelievable.

The difference between nature and civilized society lies in the social agreement that creates the ability to own, create and exchange property. The perfection of any society is in the security, accurate valuation and freedom of exchange of each individual's property.

History is full of examples of advances in understanding that have changed the world for the better. What would it have been like to watch the first person that discovered fire trying to explain it to others? What would his peers have said if he had told them that fire inside a machine could transport people and things quickly all over the earth and even to the moon and stars? Who would have believed even two hundred years ago that something as simple as a copper wire could instantly transport light, heat, sound, sight, energy and work for thousands of miles? Who would have believed even thirty years ago that every individual person would be able to communicate with any other person on earth thru tools such as email or cell phone practically anywhere instantaneously without wires?

These things could have been done at anytime in the past. The laws of the universe have not changed, only understanding was lacking. There are many more truths that have yet to be explored and discovered.

Money is an amazingly efficient tool without the interference of LCD and can be a benefit to society instead of a curse. This benefit can begin as soon as its operation is correctly understood. Here is how it works.

Chapter One

Ancient Magic

Once upon a time there was an evil wizard named Fred. Fred was evil because he wanted other people's property. In an old book of black magic and other dark arts, he discovered a spell that would make him owner of the world. The spell simply said" Lend your money at interest and spend not the increase but loan again and you will own the world." By the time Fred discovered the spell, it was already ancient. It had been used many times before, ravaging and ultimately destroying the societies that it infected. It had caused many robust ancient societies to die prolonged, pitiful and hopeless deaths. The more peaceful, civilized and trusting a society strived to be, the more prolonged and tortuous it's demise. They had been destroyed so completely that even the fragments of their history that remained bore no clue as to what caused their fate. All that was left was the old book of black magic.

Fred didn't know or care much about history but he did like the idea of owning the world. The casting of this spell was very hard on wizards; it required a determined, persistent and extremely focused necromancer to prevail.

All Fred had to his name was one gold coin. He could have spent it for breakfast, but now was time to cast the spell. He lent the coin to another person who paid Fred two coins when the agreed time had elapsed. Having lent for profit, Fred was now a lender. The two coins were lent to other people who dutifully paid Fred four coins at the end of a year. The four coins were again lent and returned eight coins. The process was repeated multiple times and after not too many years had gone by, the day came when Fred had in his hand every coin in the land.

Fred had never spent any of the interest during this time. He ate food out of garbage cans and lived in the sewer. He had a rough time. To spend all of the interest would have broken the spell and to spend even a portion of it would greatly delay the day he was waiting for when all the gold was his.

This was the simple part. Now it starts to get complicated. Through the mechanism of "Lender Created Debt" Fred had progressively achieved ownership of all of the money in the country. Even before his complete ownership of all the money, the shortage of money to perform daily business, guaranteed that the borrowers would line up at the sewer manhole to negotiate a loan from Fred. As Fred progressively consolidated ownership, the distribution, the velocity and therefore the flow of money was shifted from daily property exchange transactions to financial exchanges at the manhole.

The day that Fred achieved ownership of all of the money passed quite uneventfully. All of Fred's gold coins were loaned out again as usual and Fred disappeared with the clang of a manhole cover closing.

A year later the day to pay the loans arrived and everyone paid except one person. Fred had in his hand all of the money that he had loaned on lending day down to the last coin but he did not have the interest because there were no more gold coins in the land.

This illustrates that the process of charging interest creates debt but not the money to pay that debt. This makes the money supply and the debt a monopoly eternally at the control of the lender.

After admonishment to the nonpayer that he must work harder, Fred had the nonpayer give him a written promise to pay the gold next pay day plus the additional interest. The other customary loans were made and everyone went on their way. The next payday the former nonpayer was the first to pay Fred his debt in full. He had indeed worked very hard, neglected and deprived his wife and kids, but he had the money. Everyone else paid except two people who now did not have their payments. There was not enough gold coin in circulation to pay the additional interest that was created from the loans. Fred once again gave them a speech about hard work, sacrifice and thrift and took written promises from them to pay next time, of course with additional accrued interest. All the gold was again loaned out except to the two people who had not paid on time. After all business is business and it was quite evident to Fred that some people in the society were becoming unreliable.

The same scenario occurred again and the two former non-payers had learned a lesson and were the first to pay. Each had worked twice as hard as the average citizen, neglected their dependants but paid back their loans with interest. One had even starved his children to death accumulating enough to pay his loan. As payday concluded this time nine people could not make their payments in full. Again Fred accepted their promissory notes until the next payday.

Starving the children to death impressed Fred. He figured that anyone with that much discipline would make a good manager. The lending business had grown to the point where it required all of Fred's time to keep track of all the loans. This pattern of people being unable to pay also had to be addressed. He needed a helper. He hired the guy who had starved his kids to help him.

Fred had kept all of the loan accounts in memory but now with a helper everything had to be written down. It was too wet in the sewer for paperwork to last, so they also had to have an office. For the first time since this spell had been cast, Fred was now spending a portion of the interest that was collected. He didn't spend it all so his principle kept increasing in value every payday.

With his new employee keeping books and the interest income increasing, other new helpers had to be hired in increasing numbers. Some to assist bookkeeping and others to perform a wide variety of other tasks such as answering the phones and cleaning the now multiple offices.

With the acquisition of the first office, Fred had stopped lending the gold coins directly to the people. He would instead give the borrower a credit money note saying that it represented a certain number of gold coins in safekeeping. Of course the credit money note drew interest just like it was actual gold money. It did not matter how much gold Fred actually had in his possession, he could loan as much credit money in the form of notes as he wanted to and the people were glad to get it. This "credit money" was traded for goods and worked quite well in place of the coins. The "credit money" also had the advantage that Fred could issue as many notes as he wanted to and not be limited by the supply of gold coins that were available. Credit money also had the advantage that lack of money did not limit the business transactions in the society. The problem still remained that no matter how much credit money was loaned on lending day there was not enough money in the land to pay the additional interest debt the loans created. At least one borrower always defaulted. The society had made the transition from real money to credit money.

Another practice had been instituted where it was required that some property of the borrower was promised to Fred in case they couldn't pay their loan. The forfeited property was customarily resold with Fred giving a loan for its purchase to a person he deemed more creditworthy.

Each year a new record was set for loans being made. Anyone that wanted one and had the collateral would be granted a loan with one exception. Anyone that said anything derogatory about Fred or credit money or anyone having an opinion that Fred did not agree with, could never seem to get a loan approved.

Surprisingly after the paper note innovation and with Fred spending a portion of his collected interest on expenses, most loans were being paid on time. In fact Fred learned by watching his accounts that if he was collecting interest at 10% and loaned out 10% more in notes every year almost everyone could make their payments. And everyone had all the work that they could do and got paid well for it.

There was a problem. The people were doing great but Fred was not. The prices of all goods and services were going up. They were going up so fast that Fred was losing money. The inflation rate was as high as the interest rate that he was charging.

Fred hated inflation. More than he collected in interest had to be paid everyday to keep his employees from finding other jobs and towards expenses on his establishments.

Fred wasn't stupid. He knew that the included cost of interest and waiting for loans to be forthcoming, created inefficiencies in practically every business transaction and was the source of the inflation. Sellers simply raised their asking prices to pay their increasing raw materials, labor cost and the included interest necessary to keep enough money in circulation. They then passed these ever increasing prices on to their customers who passed them to their own customers who passed them right back to Fred. The money in the free market segment of the society took into account the actual cost of production of goods and services with included interest, and passed that cost back to Fred by way of inflation. Fred had to pay free market price for property he consumed including the cost of all of the property consumed by each of the "nonproductive tricksters" that he employed. This meant he could not simply raise the interest rate because it was causing the inflation.

Prices had to be driven down because Fred was losing money. The next page in the old book of black magic had a cure. If the society curses you with inflation do not make so many loans. At first this seemed like a bad idea. How could you make more money by lending less? If a person asking for a loan had good credit, the proper collateral and a visible means of repaying the loan why not lend them the money? Wouldn't business be done with the money, creating new goods and services, making the society richer so there would be more to take? Would not the loan be returned with interest guaranteeing a profit?

The old book said "Do not be a dope Fred. No wonder when I found you, you did not have two nickels to rub together. 10% interest return and 10% inflation plus expenses means the people will own you instead of you owning them." It was after all, a magic book.

The answer was that some people had to be made desperate enough for money that they would sell their labor for less, thereby reducing profit. Without the duress to reduce one's profit the included interest expense is passed along to the next person paying the bill which causes inflation. It worked quite well. Lending profits went up because there was not enough money in circulation for every one to work. Anyone that did have a job and asked to be paid too much was easily replaced by someone that would work harder for less. The people did not like inflation either, so when Fred told them they had to help him control it, they did so eagerly. Fred's personal "blacklist" also came in useful and was used extensively in limiting the number of loans made.

The population was now miserable. For Fred's lending business to succeed their monetary system could not be allowed to work properly. Fred's ownership of the people, everything they had or hoped to have, from the day they were born until the day they died was secured. There really was no magic after all, just Lender Created Debt.

Chapter Two

Interest Island

Interest Island is in a remote part of the ocean and has very limited contact with other people. They know that other people exist but have nothing to do with them. There are about 100 people living there. Their money supply consists of $100.00 dollars in gold coins. It is divided into many denominations so that change can be made to the nearest penny with no problem.

One day a farmer named John who grew wheat, was going home and had an accident. He dropped a present that he was taking home to his son. It was his son John Jr's birthday and the present was ruined. Another farmer named Ned saw the mishap and asked John why he didn't just buy another present. John told Ned that he had no extra money until one year from that day, when his crop could be harvested and sold. Ned told John that he would lend him the $5.00 that the present cost and that John could pay him back the $5.00 plus .50c in interest for the year.

This had never been done before, but the problem seemed to be solved. The present was purchased and the children were happy. In one year the wheat was sold and Ned was repaid. Ned decided that lending was a pretty good way to make money. He loans John the $5.50 again making the same deal for another year. In a year the $5.50 + .55c interest was duly paid back. He lends out the $6.05 again with the same terms every year because someone is always short on money. After 10 years the sum in play is $12.96. After 20 years the sum in play is $33.63. This being too much for one person to borrow, Ned is now lending to many different people. Ned is also requiring some form of collateral each time he makes a loan, just in case.

After 32 years, the total of payments owed is $105.56. On this due date, the sum that is due Ned is more than the total amount of gold coin on the island. Even people that have not been involved in the borrowing, now have the problem that if Ned decides to hold the money, no business can be done. And there is the obvious problem that on this day, Ned will not get paid unless there is a new deal made.

Let's look at what has happened before continuing with the story. For the investment of $5.00 dollars and 32 years, Ned now owns all of the money on the island. He still puts in a days work at his farm and produces as much food as he always did, takes care of his children and other obligations. He pulls his own weight in the community. The "real money" supply of the people on the island has not changed but its usage and ownership has. The money in circulation is still $100.00 in gold coins. The borrowers have to spend time managing their money to pay Ned on the due date. As these are very conscientious people, a major part of this managing consists of saving money whenever they can and buying nothing that is not absolutely necessary.

Many people who were producing products that are not absolutely necessary to life, such as birthday presents are out of business since no one has money to buy them. As the payment day approaches if the borrower has his payment in hand he must stop buying anything with that payment money. In fact as of the 31st year no prudent person could spend any money as of the day it was borrowed and reasonably predict that they could get it back by the next payment day.

There would not be enough gold to pay the interest debt accrued if all of it was lent out at the same time. The economy had become a game of musical chairs where one participant loses each time it is played. Every loan therefore had to be accepted in an act of irrational "consumer confidence" or blind ignorance. Ignorance was preferred because it required less energy for thought and the island is experiencing severe shortage of everything and everything must be conserved. This adds an element of stress and uncertainty to the community that never existed before. The money is very inefficient, and some trade must resort to barter if possible, or well established and time tested natural property exchange methods like stealing and lying.

Ned always lends them their money back and never spends any of the interest collected, so it's not like Ned is benefiting from all of this. In fact Ned is doing a lot of work that he has yet to get any benefit from. Except for the first $5.00 loan, none of this activity has benefited anyone because it is non-productive work. Most people would agree that producers should own and benefit from their labors, but to emphasize this point, this project of Ned's and the work to comply required of participants, is non-productive work. Something that is new to the community.

After 32 years Ned just happens to own all of the gold. This point in the story coming at 32 years is only important for illustration reasons. The disruption to the society would probably be so great by the 10th year something would have had to change. There would of course be many other side deals going on at any one time such as second party lending and changes in production habits creating such a confusing mess that it would defy analysis or understanding.

There are many variations the reader could envision once the basic LCD scheme is understood. Two or more people could start loaning with interest at the same time, which is very probable, private ownership of the money supply could have happened in 16 years or less. If other lenders started lending at any time, taking advantage of the "money market " that Ned has created, the 10% rate might be lowered thru competition, but with the total debt growth proceeding much faster. Even if the interest rate was lowered to 1% or less, it would have taken longer but the change in ownership in the gold money supply from public real money to private credit money would still continue as long as all of the interest is not spent.

In both the Fred the Wizard's story and Ned's tale up to now, the payment frequency was once per year, with all loans falling due on the same day. This is obviously not what happens in real life but the reader has to be able to visualize debt creation in its simplest form to understand the mechanism. If the payment day was staggered among borrowers, so that a little was borrowed and new loans were made every day, it would allow a much higher debt. Theoretically $100.00 of circulating money could be paid and reloaned each day of the year servicing a total debt of $36,500 if the interest is ignored. Interest would of course be accruing of the whole $36,500 with only $100.00 of real money in circulation. In fact, if staggered on a daily basis, depending on the velocity of money exchanged, many times more interest could be due in one year, than the value of all production and property already in existence on the island.

All that is important is the LCD principle that Ned or at least one lender somewhere in the society never spends all of the interest that he has collected so that the scheme goes on. He can spend some of it, but not all of it. If the producers in the society were in a position to charge more for their products and cause inflation, Ned would have to spend at least some of his collected interest.

The producer's ability to exchange or receive a profit on their work has been stolen. It is now dictated by what kind of mood Ned gets up with on lending day.

Up to this point, the debt created has been covered by the gold in circulation but this can no longer work. Even if Ned loans the $100.00 in gold out again the extra $10.00 to pay him the interest that would be due in course is not in existence. Something has to change, There is not enough gold. There are several things or a combination of things that could happen. Let's continue the story exploring some possibilities.

Chapter Three

Foreclosure

The due date came and during the day each debtor in turn came by Ned's house and settled his debt. It had become customary for new loans to be made on the next morning after payment day. Sam a blacksmith was the last debtor to see Ned on payment day. He told Ned he was sorry but he did not have his money which happened to be $10.00.

This took Ned completely by surprise. The tradition on this island for hundreds of years was to do what was expected of you, and this was taken seriously by everyone. This habitual reliability had been crucial to Ned's success so far. Sam had a whole year to get the money and he didn't do it. No one, not even Ned has considered that $100.00 is all of the money on the island.

Sam offers to sell Ned his blacksmith shop for $25.00 but Ned already has the shop written into the loan agreement as collateral. Ned agrees to write off Sam's $10.00 debt in exchange for the shop, and to rent it back to Sam for $2.50 per year. The remaining $15.00 of equity is forfeited to cover Ned's expenses for this inconvenience. After all business is business. The next year on payment day Sam pays his rent as required.

The $100.00 dollars that was loaned out the previous year at 10% should have brought in payments totaling $110. 00 but since there was only $100.00 in existence, now two people were short $5.00 each and another one was short $2.50, because Sam had already paid Ned his $2.50 required rent. The only thing for

Ned to do was assume ownership of these people's properties as the loan agreement stated was his right. They each rented back their former properties for $2.50, $2.50 and $1.25 per year respectively. In a few years Ned owned all of the property on the island. There was now no property in private ownership to collateralize loans with.

What could Ned do? The people had apparently forgotten how to work. They waste all of their time waiting for loan day. He was also convinced that each day, more of the people on the island were proving to be deceitful and lazy. The islands daily business was only a fraction of what it had been in the beginning. They had gone from a happy bunch of hard working, reliable people, to peons who had no time for the finer things in life.

It was every man for himself. If someone got sick they just let them die. Children had a poor chance of living until adulthood. The island was now a mean nasty dangerous place to live where all the people thought about was money. Ned didn't consider it his fault. He was just doing things that were necessary in the running of his money market such as collections, and the denying of loans when all of the gold had been loaned out for the year.

Observing the continuing disintegration of the society, he had devised a personal theory that the people were just animals and that he was the only civilized person on the island. He did too much for them. He felt he had taken care of them when they couldn't pay their bills, and felt that they despised him for it.

He got the despised part right. The people had a meeting and voted to cancel all loans and return to the original owner, property that had been taken for debt service. They set Ned adrift in a boat during a hurricane and never saw him again. Everything got better fast.

There are several points to take note of in this example.

The first is that even after all of this trouble Ned has still not yet benefited from all of this loaning and renting activity. No one on the island has benefited except that John the farmer's child received a birthday present that he might not have. The loans that were required to keep score of the property transfers necessary to the islands daily commerce were mandatory only because of Ned not spending the interest he collected.

Ned poisoned the economy and then sold the temporary antidote of more debt. Much time and effort has been wasted by Ned and everyone else in the maintaining of his "money market" scheme. It would have been better for everyone if the child had done without the birthday present.

But say instead of a present, the child needed an operation or he would die. It would have still have been better for John to steal the money from someone than to put the society through all of this trouble. Just because of the wasted time and effort over the years a lot of people in the society had to do without many things, probably many life saving operations. Even if John had killed 10 people and taken their money for the child's benefit, it would have probably been a net positive transaction for the society by a factor of 100.

The second point is, that any business plan that cannot be recommended over stealing and murder, obviously has some kind of problem and should not be promoted by civilized people, especially if few people comprehend its nature.

The third point is that after the first loan, Ned has increasing control of the total debt with each loan made. The debt can not be diminished unless he spends some of the interest money he has collected. And can never be completely paid unless he spends all interest that he has ever collected. Finally, the control becomes absolute when he owns all of the gold. The population is forced to either borrow or do no business. Thus the nomenclature "Lender Created Debt" or "LCD" accurately describes the situation.

Chapter Four

Credit money

On the next payment day, instead of canceling the debts, returning all property and waving goodbye to Ned, the people of the island make their payments as usual. They are very agitated.

That night Ned dies and all of his holdings are inherited by his son Ned Jr. His last words to Ned Jr. were "Always remember, people are animals, take care of yourself first" Ned Jr. knows the community wants answers and starts to think fast. He has never done productive work just helped Ned keep his books, and he was just now coming of age to join the productive community.

Ned had in his declining years told him many stories about how sneaky, worthless and untrustworthy the people of the island had turned out to be, and that they had to be watched all the time. Ned Jr. had learned how the scheme was managed, and had always wondered why his father didn't take some profit from all of his work. The fact was that Ned was raised a producer and lifetime habits of thrift were hard to break.

It was also his idea that his money should work as hard as he did. The money market was his hobby. He thought he was helping.

The next day everyone gathered for the meeting and after several citizens addressing the assembly, generally griping about all of the effort necessary to make the payments spoke, Ned Jr. took the podium.

Most of the older producers that had been around during Ned's time, had long since past away, and this crowd mostly consisted of their children who had taken over the family businesses. These people had never known a world without "payment day" and the following "loan it back" day. They never knew that you could buy something priced at more than a few cents without getting a loan. Since Ned passed on at midnight after payment day, this was now lending day.

As much as the public disliked payment day, loan day had turned into a day of celebration and general happiness. After a year of very exacting budgetary restraints to make sure that they each had the required gold to make their payments on payment day, loan day provided a much needed break and a time of plenty seemingly provided by Ned.

Ned Jr. had it all figured out. He stood up and started his speech. "Friends, neighbors and countrymen, we are all in this together. I know that things seem to not be running the way that they should, but since we are all in this together, if we stick together, everything can be worked out. You all knew my father and how he had a lifetime devotion to helping every one. Every one knows how he made it possible for John the farmer to not disappoint his son John Jr. by helping him replace the present that John Sr. had lost through negligence." John Jr., who was in the crowd yelled out, "That's a Fact" and the crowd cheered.

Ned Jr. continued. "There is hardly a person here that has not received a favor from my father in the form of a loan to make up for their own shortcomings or in renting them property when they lost their own through not working hard enough." Someone in the crowd remarked: "Can't argue with that." And the crowd murmured agreement. "I fully intend to honor the family tradition and pledge all of my time and resources to public service as my father, God rest his soul, has done." Someone yells: "yea for Ned Jr." and a round of applause breaks out.

"But now," says Ned Jr. "It is time to get down to the business at hand. There are many problems that must be dealt with. The gold money that has been use for so long obviously has some problems. One of the main problems is that someone might not bring in his share on payment day and cause irreparable damage to the rest of society for years to come. To address this problem for the good of everyone, and since luckily, all the gold money just happens to be at my house since yesterday was payment day, I will take it on myself to store all of it and keep it safe for every one.

" Not being able to challenge such "airtight" logic, and grateful for Ned Jrs. show of courage and selfless loyalty, by his "doing what had to be done" to halt certain disaster, the crowd cheers approval. Someone yells: "What are we going to do for money?" There is total silence, and then Ned Jr. speaks up.

"There is something that I would be willing to do at great trouble to myself but someone must do it. You all know Louis the printer who prints the bills, contracts and receipts. I will at my own expense have him print some credit money notes that correspond to the gold that is in safekeeping. He says that he has a special ink that doesn't fade and that cannot be duplicated. It will serve every purpose that the gold money did and we can even call it money. These notes will be loaned out this afternoon at the customary time and with minimal collateral required. I will trust you for repayment in one year as customary but anyone not paying on time will never get another loan because they will have proved themselves untrustworthy. And since we are in the business of solving problems today everyone will receive double the customary loan amounts requested. "

Louis printed a batch of the new money after lunch and Ned Jr. loaned it out that day at the customary 10%. It seemed that every problem was solved and everyone was happy. Business went crazy. Everyone started buying things and giving producers who had long been idle, orders for their products.

In about a month, John Jr. who had continued the family business of wheat farming was working out his budget for the rest of the year to make sure he would have the necessary money on payment day. He knew about how much wheat he could sell in that year and could see that since fertilizer and labor had already doubled in price, he would have to double his wheat price to make the required amount by payment day.

Other farmers had confronted the same facts as John Jr. and reached the same conclusion, so food prices doubled.

At the next payment day meeting the crowd was again very agitated. Since the interest rate that Ned Jr. had charged was ten percent and it was on all of the money in existence and another 10% rent on the value of all land, only about half of the people had managed to make their full payment What good does it do to have twice the money if everything cost twice as much? was the question.

Ned Jr. the man with all the answers explained the problem to them. "Although I hate to think this way, it looks like you people cannot manage your own affairs. The problem is that all of you raised your prices because you are greedy, lazy and indulge in extravagances, like birthday presents, when you should be working."

No one had actually been able to buy a birthday present for many years but each person just assumed it was a personal problem, put their best foot forward and played like everything was OK.

Ned Jr continued;" There is also the probability that someone is hoarding money and not spending it." The people had no way of knowing that Ned Jr. had gotten back every credit money note that had been loaned on the previous year. Ned Jr. continues; "From now on everyone is required to keep a written record, a "transaction report" of exactly how every dollar is received and spent or they will have to be dealt with as a criminal to society. These records will be turned into me on payment day so the criminal can be discovered.

Also these records will be used to accurately collect a 50% tax on profit to feed people who through some people's greediness can not buy food. It would be a waste of my very valuable time so I do not have to turn in a transaction report.

Excess profit has got to be controlled for the good of everyone. To this end, I happen to know that on an island not too far away from here all the wheat we can use is available for 1/20 of the price that it is here. Arrangements can be made to buy wheat from this island at this lower price to show producers here how advanced production practices can benefit everyone. Out sourcing will lower prices and leave more of our people free time for leisure."

Interest islanders did not know much about other islanders, although they knew they were there. The people on Wheat Island were a pretty rough bunch. They lived in caves if they could find one, moved to a new cave when the old one filled with refuse, did not wear clothes, did not do any work except to pick some wild wheat sometimes and pound it together with water to make wheat mush. Bones and skulls littered the ground as evidence of years of property disputes. Whose property was whose was a total mystery but it didn't really seem to matter.

The wild wheat had a flavor like sawdust mixed with used motor oil. It was kind of green in color and was covered with different kinds of insects and fungi. It grew naturally mixed in with weeds and grasses and there was a lot of it.

Since John Jr. could see that he would not sell much of the wheat that he could grow, he accepted the job of wheat importer. He went to Wheat Island with a barrel of Interest Island paper credit money to buy the first load of wheat. At first negotiations were very disappointing but John Jr. persisted.

The wheat people seemed to have no use whatsoever for the paper credit money. They had never really traded anything before and were new to the concept. When John Jr. was making one last demonstration showing how the paper notes could be licked and then stuck together to make clothes to preserve a little modesty, a breakthrough occurred.

The special ink that Louis had used had a strong garlic flavor when licked and the wheat people just loved it. When the credit money was mixed with wheat mush the flavor was indescribable. John Jr. even showed them how to bake the wheat mush on hot rocks to make a kind of bread.

With much animation, grunting, grimacing, showing of teeth and waving of hands in the air, an understanding was reached. If the wheat people would pile up enough wild wheat in his boat to fill ten barrels, John Jr. would give them the barrel of money.

Distribution back on Interest Island was without incident and everyone was delighted with the low price and abundance of wheat. A difference was quickly noticed with the first loaf of bread made. It tasted like dirty socks, would not rise and gave everyone gas. Bugs, weeds, sand and other unidentifiable organic material were found mixed together when the wheat was ground into flour. The bakers tried to pick a lot of this stuff out but the extra labor increased the price of bread so they could not afford to try too hard.

Someone complained to Ned Jr. and he just told them, "Lower prices are necessary to bring price stability back to the community, and they would learn to like the taste in time."

The complainer's name was written down in Ned Jr's records for special consideration when loan time came around again. In fact plans were being made to start the importation of what Ned Jr. termed "Wheat Island Natural Health Bread" to lower the outrageous prices the greedy bakers on the island were now asking for bread.

John Jr. could no longer afford the rent on his farm and wasn't growing any wheat anyway, so he let Ned Jr. have it back. Ned Jr. for the first time decided to spend some money on himself.

On John's old place he built a mansion and an island headquarters meeting hall. He put up a big electric fence around the whole place, had landscaping done, hired a staff to maintain and groom the place. Guards were hired with instructions to shoot anyone on sight that had no business on his property.

Anyone that worked for Ned Jr. got to wear a red hat with an N monogrammed on it. They had special privileges and were exempt from most laws. He even hired John Jr part time to grow some good wheat on a few acres in one corner just for him because he couldn't stand the Wheat Island stuff.

Let's look at what has happened.

Very soon, the several barrels of credit money that over time had been traded to the Wheat Island people for wheat, was about one half of the money that had ever been printed. On payment day 10% interest was being paid by the people of Interest Island on credit money that was no longer in existence because it had been used for flavoring on Wheat Island. Since this money was destroyed it could never be paid back and earned 10% interest forever.

Wheat and bread were still being purchased from Wheat Island because the wheat farmers and bakers on Interest Island had long been out of business and no longer had the land, shops or skill to go back into business. The interest islanders were just lucky that the money was eaten and not loaned back to them. Then they would be paying Ned Jr. interest forever and at the same time they would be paying the wheat island people interest and having to borrow even more credit money from Ned Jr. to pay that.

Ned Jr. had learned to print and loan enough credit money on loan day to cover most payments due, and to spend just enough on his own purchases to make up the difference. He had also learned to keep the money supply just short enough so that a few people would not have the money to make their payments and would exchange their labor for less, driving down everyone's wages. They could also be persecuted as examples to others, reminding everyone that payment day was what held Ned Jr's society together.

Everyone's transaction reports were also collected and put in a box in a back room. Ned Jr. could look over these reports to see how many other people were lending money at interest.

He knew that other lenders could take a part of his profit and displace him if they were allowed to accumulate significant assets. Also he knew that he would have to be sure and allow enough extra credit money to be created by additional loaning on his part so that their interest could be paid. But he also knew that the presence of other lenders was very valuable to him because they could be made sacrificial scapegoats if needed to calm an angry mob.

When Ned Jr. would lend new paper notes, money was put into the economy. When secondary lenders re-lent Ned's paper money it created velocity but no new money. The fact that secondary lenders were not allowed to print money kept them under Ned Jr's control.

He could slow down his lending activities which decreased the money supply and make them go broke at will. The interest they collect does reduce Ned Jr's interest collected but it is well worth it to him for the sacrificial shield against the angry mob of an enlightened society that they provide.

Their individual lending activities and total amount lent could be verified by the transaction reports. The reports were so complicated and tedious that no one could fill one out without at least one mistake. Two or three reports were picked at random each year and the persons filling them out were charged with some crime documented by the reports such as, omission of certain transactions or mistakes in arithmetic, as examples to the rest of society.

Although this was just the start of Ned Jr's reign, he could now buy the total production of the island in perpetuity, never giving anything in exchange except advice and paper money. He owned everything.

The people had had enough. They still had the boat that they were going to send Ned Sr off in, although it now belonged to Ned Jr. They loaded Ned Jr in his boat with all of his gold and set him adrift in the next hurricane. All loans were declared paid and all renters were given title to their property.

Production started to increase and conditions got better immediately. Since everyone was used to using credit money it was agreed to continue using it but change it into real money by distributing it equally to each member of society with no interest and to only distribute more to prevent deflation as business increased.

Chapter Five

The Lender controls the Debt

Interest is the payment of money for the privilege of owing debt for a period of time. The master lender of course specifies the interest rate, and once debt is created in a society and becomes a substantial fraction of the money supply the rules of debt change, and the lender has total control over the amount of debt in that society.

If he does not spend the interest payments, but loans them out again the debt increases. If he spends all of the interest as it is collected the debt remains constant. If he spends all of the interest that he has ever collected the debt can be paid.

If another person becomes a lender collects interest and does not spend it, the debt increases. Any number of lenders can participate in this lending market and the total debt becomes the sum of all uncollected interest plus the money in circulation minus the amount of real money that the scheme began with. In this way the lender or lenders are in absolute and exclusive control of the exact amount of debt that is earning interest in a society.

Since at any instant in time, the total debt can be described as total of interest not spent, plus money held in circulation by debt, minus any real money that was converted to credit money when the scheme started. The total debt in society is therefore caused by lending, collecting interest, on the debt, not spending the interest, and not by borrowing. The money must be borrowed or the society will be short of circulating money.

There is no such thing as frivolous borrowing in an LCD affected society. Every dollar borrowed no matter how ill advisedly spent allows a little bit of business of some kind to be done before it is sucked back into the lenders bottomless pit of debt. Once the debt in the society equals the total money in circulation, if the lender does not lend or spend the money back out as it is paid to him, the business of the society comes to a standstill. The borrower has no choice but to cooperate and forfeit whatever profit he could have made and pay whatever interest is required to stay in business.

Borrowers are clearly the heroes and have carried the torch of decency in the game of LCD. The lender can be an individual or many individuals in that society. The society becomes two separate societies with parasite/lenders forming one group and producer/ debtors forming the other. The dependants can be ignored unless they become too unruly.

A parasitic equilibrium is formed where lender/parasites consume as much of the producers profit as they can. Each time an advance in production efficiency is achieved; more lenders are created by the increased profit that results. Sometimes the lenders inadvertently consume the producer's meager profits a little faster than it can be produced and begin to consume the tools of production, producing a recession or depression. The producers produce for all of society, the debtors borrow for all of society but the lenders business is parasitic and self serving.

Money is a score keeping tool and when some people are allowed to distort the score by charging interest and promoting debt, the accuracy of the system fails, causing harm to everyone using it. Some of the problems in a society that are directly caused by LCD are:

1. Continuously rising total debt, that cannot be repaid. The nature of LCD.

2. Perpetual shortage of money to do business with. This is necessary to control inflation that would destroy the lenders.

3. Production consistently running much less than 100% so that some people cannot find work and participate in society.

This is attributable to the shortage of money to keep score of property exchange.

4. As each day goes by, every producer's profit is a progressively smaller percentage of the value of his production, particularly labor producers. Since a producer makes his living by producing he must constantly produce faster or reduce his profit or both, to stay in the negative sum game played against other producers.

5. People who cannot find work or can no longer make ends meet on what they are paid are turned into dependants. The end result of playing a negative sum game.

6. More of each producers already diminished pay is stolen by taxation to support the growing ranks of dependants. Hungry people have a limited respect for contracts. Starving people have none.

7. Dependants children are raised on the fringe of society, deprived of many of the fulfilling opportunities that a societal contract offers.

8. Some people have to resort to natural property transfer methods, (theft, lying and murder), because of the shortage of money.

9. More resources have to be devoted to law enforcement to prevent natural property transfer. (theft, lying murder or whatever)

10. Division of society into two distinct groups, lenders and producers whose goals in life are as different as tigers and lambs.

11. The producers that are able aspire to become lenders because it is perceived that there is more stability in the lending business than in any productive business.

12. The producers that are left have to cut every corner that they can and give up all profit to the point of bankruptcy to stay in business. They have to come as close as legally allowed to cheating their customers to stay in business.

13. Laws have to be constantly updated to keep pace with advances in fraud.

14. Government has to collect more taxes every day and when these taxes are insufficient, violate the trust of the people by participating in natural property transfer enterprises, such as a multitude of fines and fees. Government is forced to proceed with a socialist agenda to manage the collateral damage that the lenders generate. Members of the government use whatever power their office gives them to enrich themselves and their friends. Justice in the society can be bought or thwarted through payments to government, either under the table or by penalties and fines.

15. Lenders have to spend increasing percentages of their own profits to maintain their lending and collection activities. Even though this can seemingly provide employment, all of this labor is non-productive and of no benefit to society since its only purpose is to keep the nonproductive lenders in business.

Effort spent controlling any specific problem or symptom of the underlying "Lender Created Debt" provides only temporary relief and results in more debt either from the relieved person having some more money to loan or more collateral to pledge. For example if a new method of tax collection that is more efficient than the one currently used were implemented, there would be more money in the hands of secondary lenders who would loan it out thereby increasing the total debt and the interest payments collected. Lenders would benefit but not society.

LCD always advances until misery stops its progress. The most often suggested cure of reducing taxes provides a little instant prosperity which is quickly absorbed by increases in lending.

Simple debt is a simple concept. One person needs some property that another person has. He borrows that property for an agreed amount of time. At the end of that time the property is returned to the lender with an additional amount of property or "interest" as the lenders profit for making the loan. This simplicity rests on a foundation of assumptions. The lender assumes that the borrower intends to and has the capability to repay the agreed amount. The borrower assumes that he will receive fair market value for any production he does and therefore makes the judgment that he can repay the loan. He also makes the assumption that there is a sufficient market for his production to repay the loan. Above all each party assumes that the other party is acting in good faith and not lying or hiding some fact that would affect either party's decision. They also both assume that there is a sufficient amount of property, or money, to pay the debt. If this last assumption is incorrect the simple debt becomes LCD.

Simple debt can be beneficial to a society because it does serve the function of making some property available for production in certain instances where that particular property is temporarily unavailable. The opposite of simple debt is total debt that requires a new loan be obtained and more interest promised every time anything is purchased no matter how small.

"Lender Created Debt" has two characteristics that differentiate it from the "simple debt" model that most people understand.

Number One: LCD can only be repaid when the lenders of the society allow its repayment by spending all of the interest that has been received to date. Unless the interest created by debt is spent, it can only be paid by another loan which of course buys time but ultimately increases the debt. Interest therefore accrues in perpetuity and the debt increases out of the control of the borrower. The name "Lender Created Debt" originates from the fact that once a debt becomes "Lender Created Debt", the only source of funds available to the debtor for the repayment of that debt is from the proceeds of an additional loan that creates new debt, thereby "compounding" the debt. The lender is essentially hoarding the interest to make it more valuable and more in demand.

LCD first manifests itself on the personal, usually described as the micro level. The personal symptoms are rather vague and are usually attributed to personal failings. Some people can't seem to find jobs, presumably because they are lazy. The actual monetary compensation for people with employment progressively diminishes and many things that were affordable previously like one parent staying home and raising the kids become scarcer every day. Its diagnosis and identification at this level without the knowledge of the monetary state of the rest of the society is extremely difficult. A definitive diagnosis of societal or macro LCD is possible when the total free money supply, in a society, is insufficient to pay in full the outstanding debt of that society on any given date. Although symptoms may have been manifesting themselves well before the definitive diagnosis stage, proof in the micro case is difficult. "Lender Created Debt" is usually mistaken for simple debt, where the debtor simply pays the creditor the amount of the original loan plus a pre-agreed amount of interest in consideration for the making of the loan. To be a simple debt, the total debt in the society must be small in relationship to the money in circulation that is available to pay it. Total debt can probably be no more than 5% of the money supply without causing distortions in pricing, inflation and money availability.

Number Two: Both LCD and simple debt cause inflation. As the interest associated with any debt, LCD or simple, is included in the cost of goods and services in the LCD society, the average price level necessarily goes up. Ordinarily .25c flour plus .25c heat plus .25c labor plus .25c profit would equal $1.00 for a loaf of bread. Under LCD conditions .25c flour plus .25c heat plus .25c labor plus .25c profit plus .05 for interest plus .20c for externality control would total $1.25 for a loaf of bread. Also a portion the velocity of the money supply is wasted changing hands from lenders to borrowers. This necessitates an increase in credit money supply with its associated interest expense to be added to the total.

Simple debt does not exist in a society in sufficient quantity without becoming LCD to cause much inflation. Therefore most inflationary tendencies in a society may be attributed to management of LCD.

Lenders can only tolerate a certain level of inflation because it can cancel out the gains that they receive from their interest payments. The way that inflation is reduced to a level acceptable to the lenders is to reduce the money supply that is available to do the societies business, thereby creating a deflationary condition. This also increases the demand for loans and therefore the interest rate that can be charged for additional loans.

The fact that many individual productive opportunities are lost because there are shortages of money to do business is incorrectly attributed to greediness and failings of the free market or capitalism.

Every additional loan increases the rate of transfer of money ownership in the form of interest payments, from the productive members of society to the non-productive lenders.

Enough money is loaned into the society to maintain a level of production, but not enough for everyone in that society to do all of the business that is necessary. The phenomenon that this practice creates could properly be termed "transactional exclusion" since it creates a dependant segment of the LCD society that is deprived of enough efficient business transactions to supply their needs or the needs of their children. They can work all they want too they just can't get fairly paid.

As the duration of the "transactional exclusion" becomes multigenerational, a permanently deprived segment of society develops that has been effectively denied participation in the benefits of society through out their development. This includes education in skills that makes them productive members of the society.

After a certain amount of deprivation, education is a poor investment because the person has permanent damage. Even if they could be trained in a skill to be more productive their only option is to accept work for less money throwing someone else out of a job. A lot of the time is better to just feed the dependants so they don't get mad.

It is important to note that these excluded citizens did not have to be either debtors or creditors to be subject to these continuing damages. They constitute a damaged sector of society. Because of the lender-debtor activity going on there simply can not be enough money in free circulation for them to fully participate in society.

These deprived citizens have good reason to hold a grudge against the lenders of society for the exclusion that caused and continues to guarantee their plight. This animosity is misdirected at anyone who is better off monetarily or seemingly "rich" rather that the lenders who are actually to blame.

For every dollar that is collected by a lender the transactionally excluded dependants of the society probably lose twenty. Much of the dependant's loss can not be estimated in monetary terms. For instance, what compensation could be given to a person for not being able to supply food, housing and education to their own children? The child grows up believing that his parents are failures, lazy and deficient. How much compensation would it be appropriate to pay a person one week before he died to makeup for a life spent waiting for handouts and not being able to have the satisfaction of being a productive member of society.

A different set of lifestyle skills are necessary to be a dependant rather than a producer. These skills are what the children learn by example, I repeat example, not handouts, while observing their parents level of participation in society. They learn the rules and skills of the game that is being played, even if their roll in that game is to sit on the bench. The average jungle tribesman could not be chairman of the board of some corporation. And the average CEO would probably be short lived by himself in the jungle. Not because of intelligence but because of a heritage of training and experience.

Deprived of thousands of years of knowledge, social evolution begins anew with each generation. All of the old mistakes have to be remade and old social technology reinvented. Idle dependants engage in ancient elementary social experiments such as theft or gang associations in an effort to supply property acquisition and security that is denied them by exclusion from mainstream society.

Governments of modern societies usually tax the productive members of society to provide minimum education, food and health care to the deprived classes so they do not get agitated enough to try to address their problem with ignorant, antisocial and violent acts that disrupt the flow of interest payments to the lenders. They constantly remind the dependants that they are undeserving of this handout.

This transfer from the producers to the dependants lends an undeserved air of respectability to the government. It makes it look like it really cares about the less fortunate in society and obscures the fact that they are cooperating with the lenders to cause the damages.

Any government's right to tax is derived from the necessity of supplying public goods to the society. Redistribution of property from those that have it to those who need it, for the purpose of minimizing ongoing damage caused by lenders is not a function of an honest or trustworthy government. The compensation for the damaged dependants should come directly from taxes on the lenders not the producers. If the government was supplying an efficient system of currency in the first place, as a public good, the dependant problem would be almost nonexistent.

This practical necessity of a perpetual shortage of money and the included cost of interest results in all property transactions in the LCD society to be inaccurate and all actual producers to be underpaid, some worse than others. Those who can stay productive even if they are underpaid are luckier than the dependants. For every dollar in interest collected by the lending segment of society the productive class probably loses three.

What LCD does not do is supply money and property to where it is needed in society. The well worn theory, justification and excuse for lending in general, is that it supplies the right property at the right time for the efficient production of more property. The theory and justification of collecting interest is that the lender defers his use of the money until later, so that more efficient use may be made of the property it can buy by another. It is a simple assumption that he should get the money back at some date plus a portion of the surplus produced by the loan.

This simple assumption assumes a lot. It first assumes that the loan is not a product of duress such as the requirement to pay the interest on a previous loan. Secondly it assumes that the lender community has not had a hand in reducing money supply thereby increasing the necessity of a loan. The third assumption is that the property/money was lent for a productive endeavor. If a gun is lent to another to harvest animals for food, the lender should have the benefit of being fed also. If the same gun was lent to perform a robbery and a third party is killed, the lender shares in the new collateral debt created. Even if the lender and borrower get away with a profit because no one can collect the collateral debt, society is degraded by the act.

Lender created debt has this net effect, since so much collateral damage, or negative externality as the economist would say, is caused by the required shortage of money, the act of loaning a little property to where it is needed for a productive project can never yield a return to society.

These twenty steps should help clarify the progression of LCD.

1. Money is lent at interest.

2. Money plus interest is repaid.

3. None of the money or interest is spent but is lent again.

4. Steps 2 and 3 repeat

5. The sum of principle plus accrued interest is equal to the sum of all money in the society.

6. Lender begins to create money notes to lend at interest to compensate for shortage of real money.

7. Steps 2 and 3 repeat with some but not all of the interest being spent for lenders expenses.

8. Commerce flourishes due to availability of money to keep score of property transactions.

9. Lender allows anyone holding money to lend it at interest.

10. Inflation caused by the cost of interest embedded in every transaction that up until now had been controlled by a shortage of money is now manifested.

11. Lender limits the issuance of his own notes to offset the inflation by creating deflation caused by a lack of circulating money.

12. Lack of money in society reduces number of secondary lenders that hold enough money to lend.

13. Many people can not obtain enough money to perform enough production to provide for their living requirements.

14. Government, who has been complacent in this lending progression, steals money from producers and gives it to starving dependants to quell riots.

15. The sum of principle plus unspent interest climbs to several times the sum of all money in the society.

16. Advances in productivity promise more products for everyone.

17. Productivity increases materialize but are absorbed by increased activity of secondary lenders creating more interest bearing loans and therefore more interest caused inflation.

18. Managing lenders reduce note creation to reduce number of weaker secondary lenders causing recession for lack of money.

19. Managing lenders increase issuance of notes allowing manifestation of inflation.

20. Steps 17,18and 19 repeat indefinitely.

Chapter Six

Public Goods

Certain property by its nature does not provide efficient benefit to society if it is allowed to be privately owned. This type of property is known as a public good property. Some examples of public goods are the air we breathe, sunshine to grow food, social contract agreements to secure personal property rights, laws to define those rights, law enforcement service to ensure each persons property rights, roads to enhance convenience in travel and a monetary system to promote efficient property transfer.

A society's government's responsibility is the management of public goods for the maximum benefit of every person in that society. If members of the government can be bribed to create laws benefiting one special person or group, the government can not be trusted by the people in the society. The selling of a public good for private profit is impossible without the cooperation of the government.

So much of the operation of money in a society is hidden from view, except when involved in an actual transaction, that it is hard for anyone to really understand what is happening. Let's take a public good such as the road system and see what happens when it is converted from public to private ownership.

Imagine that one day someone was driving down a road somewhere and was thinking about things. One of the things that he was thinking about was who owned the road. After several theories were considered, he came to the conclusion that since he was paying no one for the use of the road that it must be his. He stops in the middle of the road and tells the car behind him that they may not proceed until he is paid a fee. The people in the other car had never heard of such a fee, but paid it because who would lie about something like that.

The news spread fast. Anyone could stop in the road, park and charge any one else a fee to drive on the portion of the road that they had claimed ownership of. Someone complained to the legislature and they responded that a law had never been made to deal with such a situation. They promised that the issue would be brought up next session.

A representative whose relatives were making a living charging driving fees, brought forth a bill entitled, Regulation of Public Roads for the Good of Society. This bill stated: Road use fees may only be collected by a driver with a duly issued road use fee collection license. There could be only one road use fee collection station every 200 feet of travel. All road use fees charged will be set by a fee setting governing board and every road use fee would be subject to a 50% tax payable directly to the governing board. The Governing Board is hereby granted the authority to hire as many administrators, assistants, clerks, inspectors and other employees as they deemed necessary to regulate the fee system. This bill was law by the end of the day.

The governing board which was composed of people, who made their living charging road use fees, issued licenses to favored applicants and published a daily guide to maximum fee rates allowed on different roads. The Governing Board used the tax income to pay for their expenses, salaries, retirement plans, medical plans, performance bonuses, a fleet of helicopters and planes so they wouldn't get stuck in traffic and many new headquarters and district offices befitting the importance of their duties in society.

All highway maintenance was performed by the government highway department and paid for by a tax on fuel as it had been for years. The tax of course had to be doubled because less fuel was purchased because of reduced travel and the road use fees made transportation of the road building materials more expensive.

The privatizing of the roads for the collection of fees had a dramatic effect on the society. While the price of the toll was substantial, the real problem was the amount of time it took to travel and transport goods because of all the starting and stopping.

Trips that use to take 1 hr now could take 100 hrs. People that used to be able to take care of themselves and earn their own living could not afford the trip to and from their job, and had to beg for a living or die. The government of course had to increase taxes to aid people who could not earn a living.

The cost of any product or good could now be described as Labor + Material +Profit + Cost of Transportation = Price, with Cost of Transportation being about 50% of the total price of everything and climbing.

Many benefits were of course claimed for the fee system. It provided work albeit unproductive, for a lot of people since one in three occupations were now related to the toll system. Other industries developed, supplying specialized goods and services to the fee collectors, such as money collecting and accounting services to comply with the Governing Boards tax requirements.

What was wasted on replacing brake shoes was compensated for in reduced fuel usage, mostly because many people could not afford to travel at all. It reduced speeding because the average distance between stops was 200 feet.

As years went by people could not even remember what life and work was like before movement fees. They knew they were probably necessary because they provided so many jobs.

This absurd example of converting a public good into private property is accurate in many respects in comparison to the problem of public money or any public good being converted to private gain.

The money be it gold or paper, is already in use and its maintenance cost are being borne by productive members of society. The interest cost charged for the use of the money, like the road fee charges, is almost insignificant compared to the inefficiency of property transfer and production that its implementation, collection and debt management, causes in the society.

The parasitic special interest group that benefits and controls what should be a public good becomes an antisocial organization. Public good conversions, and the people that benefit from them, are non-productive and are parasites on society. The often repeated justification of money lending, that it allocates "capital" when and where it can best be used in the society can be readily countered by the argument that for every $1.00 supplied at the right time $100.00 has been lost through inefficiency. Sellers of other people's property being predatory/ parasitic in nature do not care if someone else loses $100.00 as long as they collect their $1.00. The lenders are selling score keeping liquidity and the fee collectors are selling road access and there is now less availability of each product for everyone.

The solution is simple in both cases. Outlaw the fee collecting and the interest collecting or tax them to compensate their victims and return the public goods, the roads and money, to their proper owners, the public.

Chapter Seven

The Path to a Civilized Society

Trees have property, bears have property, ants have property, amoebas, snails, snakes, fish, gophers, grass, birds, mold, fungus, horses, dogs, and cats have property. It would be better to say they wish they could have property. In nature each entity has to protect its own property as best it can with no outside help. Anyone can take this property anytime they can get away with it, and it would not even be considered stealing. This is the wonderful world of nature and "Natural Property Transfer".

Any particular organism in nature has two primary goals; reproduction and the acquisition of needed property to sustain life. Every organism in existence is essentially an experiment in how to construct a living thing so that it can acquire the property it needs when it is needed and keep it long enough to use it. In the millions of years of experimentation, cooperation between organisms has proved to be vastly superior to all others in the acquisition, security and even creation of property. Even the concept of property is a result of this promising experiment.

In nature, property that some production has been done to usually has greater value. Most of the production in nature is personal production, or the growing and reproduction of the organism. Trees take water and minerals out of the soil, sunlight and oxygen out of the air and produce leaves seeds and wood. Grass takes the same raw materials and makes more grass. Animals eat grass and leaves and make meat and baby animals. Some animals eat other animals and so on.

Natural property transfer is paid for not in money but in "Havetos". Force and deception, or both, are used by all living things in nature to create "Haveto" traps. Force and deception involve the taking of property without regard for any theory of ownership by other organisms. In fact, nothing in nature gives even the slightest thought to taking property except maybe whether it can get away with it. NPT does not consider what collateral damage that the taking of certain property might do to another living thing. Every time a tiger eats, something has to die. How many things have to die to supply a tiger for his lifetime? Say a tiger lives thirty years and kills something to eat every day, that's $30 \times 365 = 10950$ or an externality factor of $10952/1$.

All living organisms develop defense strategies for keeping the property that they already have. With the prospect of losing enough property not to be able to sustain life and reproduction, it is a subject that cannot be ignored. Even this necessity of defense constitutes another externality and consumes additional resources.

Practitioners of natural property transfer do not care how much collateral damage is caused by any action they take. It is not a part of the natural equation. This makes the natural world a very unfriendly place to live, quite contrary to idealistic views of nature. There are a lot of things to be learned from nature but friendship, love and kindness are not to be found except sparingly in some social animals.

Several thousand books could be written on this subject and not describe every technical intricacy in natural property transfer. Needless to say in the millions of years that have passed before this book was written, almost every combination of force and deception has probably been tried countless times with varying rates of success. It is easy to recognize some of the more successful combinations, as the practitioners are still alive. Also it goes without saying that a lot of property has been naturally transferred since time began.

Property is not secure without a social contract. Predators and parasites whether they are animal or human operate outside of social contract. Under a social contract it is well defined and understood that taking of property by force or deception is an offence against the victim, and the perpetrator is a criminal. It is understood that the use of necessary force in the protection of property is acceptable and beneficial to a civilized society.

Also it can be seen that if any productive member of society is threatened with natural property transfer, the whole of society is affected because that individual's productive contribution to society is wasted planning contingencies to prevent his property from being stolen. It is far better for all of society to let the producers produce, instead of standing guard over their property.

A society formed by enlightened people using a bi-lateral agreement as the foundation of all rule of law can exhibit extremely high efficiencies of production. The basic agreement looks something like this.

I will not steal your property if you will not steal mine, and I will not let anyone steal your property if you will not let anyone steal mine. Anyone is welcome and everyone is invited to join in this contract. This is loosely known as republicanism.

Under this contract citizens of the society can own, and be secure in their ownership of their own property. Each one contributes a portion of their production to pay for the upkeep and management of public goods thru a system of taxation. The government works for the benefit and derives it's authority from the citizens. Individual representatives may be voted out if they exhibit antisocial behavior in the performance of their duties. The primary duty of this type of government is the establishment and management of public goods.

The tricky part in this form of government is establishing the dividing line between what should be personal property and what should be public property.

Several factors contribute to the efficiency of production in this system. One is that since each person may keep the property that he produces to enhance the quality of life, there is great incentive to produce a lot of high quality property. Another is that each individual may specialize in the production of a certain type of property and invest time and effort in maximizing skills particular to that type of production. Yet another very important factor is that the individual has the right to say no to a transaction if it is not in his interest. If he believes property that another person is offering him for a trade is not being represented accurately He just says no to the exchange. This has the effect of making truth more valuable than lies in the process of obtaining property. This is in direct contrast to the natural system. A good lie in a natural property transfer system is a valuable property in itself. If people can cooperate in establishing truth a lot of it can be found. This system is so efficient and works so well that the citizens tend to get lazy.

All forms of government except pure socialism are vulnerable to takeover by LCD. Once LCD runs its course the social contract changes from "don't take my property and I will not take yours", to "do not do anything that harms the lenders property". This schism that divides the society into lenders that own everything and producers that do all of the productive work, makes a joke out of the social contract so it falls into disuse.

An efficient means of valuing and exchanging property is as important as property security itself. If every time property is exchanged half is lost to a third party through monetary inefficiency, it has the same effect as half of the property being stolen. If some people are overpaid for a non productive activity there will be a lot of that activity. Also if an exchange can not take place in a timely manner because of a lack of money, some property does not get produced because a producer's time is wasted.

The republican bi-lateral contractual system is the most sensitive to the quantity and management of money in that system. Since no property exchange takes place without money, all property is theoretically valuated and accounted for. As the producers are more specialized there has to be more transfers of different types of property between them. In this society natural property transfers are not allowed because it wastes the producer's time. Barter is too slow for many reasons, every exchange has to be of equal value and it is cumbersome to make change.

Money increases the efficiency of transfer over barter since it is a superior method of keeping score of the quantity and the value of each producer's property. When money supply is low, in relation to the property transfers that need to be accomplished each day, all possible beneficial transfers simply do not happen. Take away the benefits of the money system and natural transfer has to be resorted to for people to obtain needed property. Property can be paid for or stolen or a mixture of both. Paying is civilized and stealing is natural. No matter how conscientious and productive each producer is, the property produced is worthless if he cannot use it himself or exchange it for property he can use.

Chapter Eight

How Money Works

Understanding real money and how it aids property transfer is really very easy. In any society that has enough of a social contract in place to allow some free time for productive activities and resulting trade, some form of money develops in the course of doing business. It is usually some commodity that has almost universal value in that community such as grain, livestock or metals. It is also generally something that has a stable or predictable supply and demand so that it can be self calibrating.

Money is not value. It is data. It is information about the relative worth at a certain point in time of any particular property to any particular buyer. It automatically factors in such diverse data as how much of a particular property is being produced, how many people want it and how bad, what it costs in labor, material and other inputs to produce. All that information is included in the price the instant that a price between buyer and seller is agreed upon.

Part of moneys great usefulness is that it provides a common denominator for trading property of wildly different kinds and establishing quickly and with an amazing degree of precision, the value and ownership before and after transfer of different kinds of property. While two barterers are discussing whether a cow is worth two or three sheep, an efficient money system can tell you to within one penny exactly how much a cow or a sheep is worth to each party. It can also tell you what they were worth yesterday and what they will probably be worth tomorrow. When the seller's valuation is less than the buyer's, a sale is possible.

The other attribute assigned to money is that it is a store of value. If the money is honestly calibrated this is true for an individual or subset of society, but not society as a whole. Money is of course worthless as a store of value especially long term if there is LCD involved with its inherent inflation.

Doubling the amount of money in a society does not make it richer unless there is a preexisting a shortage of money in circulation to do business with. If every person in the world had a ton of gold coins but there was no food, it is probable that everyone would starve. If some people had food and would accept gold coins in exchange for it there might be the basis for some business.

Money ownership signifies that its owner has given to another person some property and is due some back. The money having some intrinsic value or usefulness in its own right can be a safe guard of its durable precision. For instance, if the money was wheat or some other food substance, it could be eaten if no one wanted to take it in trade for another product. Gold or other metals can be used to make all sorts of useful products.

The total quantity in circulation in all of society does not make the society richer or poorer but a change in quantity does produce inflation or deflation. For instance, if a cow based money economy got hungry and ate some of their cows, they would be short on cow money. Cow money would be scarcer and therefore more valuable relative to other property and prices would fall.

The same would happen if aluminum was chosen as a standard. Someone could develop a cheaper method of production greatly increasing the supply and prices would rise because the money would be worth less per pound. The money would still work, but society would waste time adjusting to the new prices. As some people are separated from their property for less than it is truly worth and some people benefit from the windfalls created, temporary inefficiencies of transfer would be introduced.

Money is a system of exchangeable tokens that represent value. A good definition of money is that it is a universally agreed upon and recognized token that provides a mathematical model facilitating accuracy in determining of value and keeping score of ownership of property.

For these functions of valuation and score keeping to correctly model reality, at least three factors must be controlled. First, included expense should be kept to an absolute minimum. This means interest, included interest, passed on interest or excessive seigniorage fees.

Second, the amount in circulation should be calibrated so that inflation and deflation is minimized.

Third, there should be minimum duress involved in the transaction especially if in the form of havetos created by special interest groups.

Although there are many examples of intrinsic value commodity monies in history, metals, especially silver and gold are the most used. These metals have relatively stable production compared to their demand and are easily divisible into coins of a value to make trading convenient.

For money to measure and store value with maximum efficiency, the money must be calibrated or standardized as with any other measurement tool. This is accomplished somewhat automatically in an evolved intrinsic money system due to only a finite amount of money token material being available. Its relative scarcity limits how fast new supplies are found and mined so that this slow addition to the total stock roughly parallels the growth of population and the money seems to calibrate itself. Gold and silver coins are of course an example of automatically calibrating money tokens. This natural self calibrating feature is deceptive, and fools many people, in that it appears to be a dependable characteristic of intrinsic money. The self calibration only works in the simplest of economies and can easily be overwhelmed by rate of growth, imbalance of trade with foreign economies or interest expense. When all of the gold and silver is owned by Ned or Fred and resides in their vaults it is obviously not calibrated anymore.

Credit money is not self calibrating because it can be created instantly in any quantity desired. In the simplified Fred and Ned examples it could be imagined that even though each could produce credit money notes at will, they would also learn through experience to moderate note issuance to control inflation. This feedback does not work in a multi-lender multi-note creator society. The individual note creators would each endeavor to maximize their own profits by over issuing their own notes. There has to be a system of cooperation between the multiple lenders in a society.

Chapter Nine

Money X Velocity = Price X Quantity

If there are 100 one dollar bills in circulation in a society, and each one is spent on average once a week, in a year of 52 weeks there would be $5200.00 dollars worth of business done. If there were 200 one dollar bills in circulation in the same society an each one was spent on average once every two weeks, the same $5200 dollars worth of business would be done. If the rate of spending were increased to the original one time per week and there were still 200 dollar bills in circulation $10400.00 dollars worth of business would be done in that year.

This simple relationship is poorly understood by most people. It is basic to understanding how money operates in a society. For example if one person in the society owned and held one half of the money out of circulation instead of spending it, the rest of society would have to increase their velocity or lower prices to do the same amount of business. The same price lowering or deflation would happen if the size of the society doubled without any increase in the money in circulation.

It is also important to understand that a certain number of property trades must occur each day for every person to work, purchase their raw materials, produce and get paid. So to go back to the example of one person holding one half of the money, if the velocity cannot be increased the prices must be reduced by half. This would at first seem like a good deal for every one. Bread was $1.00 and is now is .50c, gas was $2.00 a gallon and is now $1.00, and new houses cost $50,000 instead of $100,000. The catch is that pay is also cut in half, if a person used to make $10.00 per hour they now make $5.00, if they use to make $2000.00 per month they now make $1000.00. But even with this scenario the money in existence after a short time of adjustment still efficiently and accurately facilitates the necessary business. When the person starts to spend the money that he is holding, prices again increase back to the original state. Another possible scenario would be that if gold were being used as money, say .05c, .10c, .25c, .50c, $1.00, $10.00 $20.00,ect coins, enough new gold would be found that when turned into coins, would double the amount in circulation. After some adjustment period, the average price of everything would double. Because of the increased supply a pound of gold would be worth one half what it was before. The average business done would not change unless there had been an unnatural shortage of money in the first place.

In the Wizard and Interest Island examples all of the velocity is initially that of real money exchanged in daily trade. At the time that the LCD lender or lenders acquire ownership of the society's money supply the velocity is almost exclusively that of borrowing, lending and loan repayment. Credit money then has to be continuously created so that it can be exchanged in daily business transactions.

In a basic intrinsic real money system the commodity that is used as the money has to be in reasonably stable supply. Although there is usually some production and development of new reserves that gradually add to the money in circulation, the increase is balanced by an increase in population.

Productivity in a society can increase through sophistication of technology. This sophistication usually takes the form of increased specialization in skills better understanding of the nature of each process and more efficient production techniques. This specialization necessitates more trading or transactions being done on a daily basis. As a result of this "division of labor" and the increased efficiency of production, the price factor decreases and the quantity of property supplied factor increases.

Velocity is the average of how many times one unit of money is spent during a year. It could also be stated as how many times the whole money supply is spent during a year. The most important factor affecting velocity is how much money a person holds in reserve against future needs.

A person for example might know that he will need to buy $50.00 dollars worth of food before the next time he gets paid, and will save that much in reserve so he will not go hungry. He does not spend it as soon as he gets it but holds the money for a time to purchase food when it is needed. He also does not immediately buy enough food because of the need for storage and type selection would have to be address at once. Increased flexibility in the face of an uncertain world has value. If the food is bought as it is consumed he has a wider variety of choice.

A person could also be saving for longer term goals such as an unexpected illness, to buy a house or to retire in later years. This "saved" money waiting to be spent on future needs greatly lowers the average velocity of each individual dollar. The effect of having many people holding their money and not immediately spending and consuming that which they produced the day before has a beneficial deflationary effect on the society. The price is lowered for people that need goods now. The cost of new tools of production such as factories, machines and public goods infrastructure such as roads, bridges, education and defense is lowered so that more is demanded and more is produced. This benefit is because of real saving and not by frenzied LCD activity.

The biggest factor on velocity once LCD has infected a society is the non productive activity of making and paying back of loans. For example consider a farmer that takes his crop to town, sells it for $10.00 buys seeds and other supplies and goes home and begins the next years work.

Under LCD he would sell the crop for $10.00. This being just the amount necessary to pay his outstanding $9.00 loan plus interest. He then borrows $15.00 to buy the next years seeds and supplies because prices have gone up. If he is lucky he can get the loan on the same day buy his supplies and go home. If the lender is not lending that day because he is limiting loans to control inflation, the farmer will have to take his place in line and wait for his turn. This could take from one day or until next year or never. After all lending to a farmer that does not have a crop in the field especially after several years is a questionable risk.

Price is the most volatile variable in the MV=PQ equation. This is good because what we want efficient money to do is quickly and accurately measure the value of any property in question.

In addition to being affected by changes in M,V and Q as described in the preceding discussion, there are several components that combine together to form the price of any given property. The most important three are raw materials, labor and profit. This could be described as material plus labor plus profit equals price. Even materials found lying on the ground or growing in nature require picking up and transporting some distance to be of use. So labor would be added to the cost of these supposedly free materials.

Another possibility is that another person acquires the property from the gatherer and improves it in some way such as making a rock into an arrowhead or cooking some item to create tastier food.

The more specialized any type of labor is, the more the addition of profit becomes important to retain a part of the value of the improved property to each individual producer. The price for a given item of property and indeed if it will sell at all, is also affected by the price of another property that will serve the same purpose as the original. If one establishment sells hamburgers for $2.00 each, it would be hard for another place across the street to sell the same quality hamburger for $20.00. The higher price that someone will actually give for a certain property the less is the chance that some other property will serve the exact purpose as the original.

Another important concept in price is who actually pays. If in making a hamburger the cook buys meat and buns, the price paid for the raw materials and the labor and profit that went into making of the meat and buns is passed along to the person that eats the hamburger. If the person is a dependant child who does not have any money to pay for the hamburger, then some producer, usually a parent, has to exchange some of their production for money to pay for it. The cost of anything is always paid by the person who does not or can not pass it to someone else. This person invariably turns out to be a producer because producers are effectively the source of all property. This "cost pass along" effect can get quite complex in the real world, but elementary money can keep accurate score of all the transactions.

Real money does not have to get its value from being made of gold or other commodity. Even a piece of paper can be made valuable and become money by a contract between parties in the society. The money's value comes from its reliability of calibration to the business of the society and its usefulness in modeling the value of property value in the society. The money creation contract would specify that the paper real money represents property value and that no individual can produce the real paper money, and that a stable supply of the paper real money should be managed for the convenience of every member society. Provisions also have to be made to define, detect and control fraud in the issue and distribution of the paper money.

The most important consideration with money is how it is put into circulation. There are three main ways to get paper money into the hands of the people of the society.

1. Distribute it equally to each individual member of society.

2. Spend it in.

3. Loan it in.

What has given paper real money a bad reputation is that the people in charge of distribution always give in to the temptation to spend or loan it in. Either method defrauds the society and makes parasites of the group doing the distribution. Both the spenders and the lenders get property for free without themselves producing any thing of value. Then they quickly come to the realization that if they spent or lent the money in once, they can do it again. All of their waking hours and efforts are spent in the repetition of their new trick. Printing and spending new paper money into circulation is so obviously fraud that the spenders usually attempt to confuse the issue with claims the money is backed by gold, land, other paper assets or their own well deserved faith and credit.

Lenders usually require the borrowers to supply their own assets as collateral and therefore supply the value for the money issue while the lenders get the interest payments free and clear. Either way the producers need the money so bad, no matter how tainted or compromised it is, to keep score of production, they agree to whatever terms are demanded.

Distribution of new money directly to each member of the society as needed to calibrate the total money supply for growth or other changes in society defrauds no one and creates no conflict of interest within the issuing authority.

It should go without saying that the price of an item is used by anyone in judging the value of that particular property. With the value of different properties known, decisions can be made as to how much one's own production is worth. This determines how much of some one else's production can be acquired. Accurate decisions can be made about activities such as changing jobs for higher pay or the utilization of new methods of manufacturing that might be more efficient.

If the value of the money is affected by its method of distribution or included cost such as interest, there is a pre-existing inaccuracy in all decisions of the society. Price as the sum of material plus labor plus profit equals price, instead becomes, material plus labor plus profit plus cost of money equals price. The cost of money includes interest cost, opportunity cost and the cost of damage control of the lender created externalities.

An inadequate quantity of total transactions has the potential to cause much damage. Imagine there are 10 producers that work all day at their individual jobs and at the end of the day their respective tasks are complete. They have all made products that each other want. The next morning because of LCD money manipulation there is not enough money for 5 of them to sell their entire product and buy the materials that are required for this days work. Today only half as much is produced as yesterday not because of skill or willingness to work but because the goods produced can not be exchanged.

These transactionally challenged people can not buy food so the other producers share their food with the hungry because they are decent people. This creates a food shortage in the able to produce group so they do not get as much done. Every work day becomes a game of frantic "musical chairs" chasing what money is available.

This brief discussion of economic theory is only intended to illustrate the author's reasoning supporting some of the opinions that are put forth. It is highly recommended that the reader does additional study and acquires some background in economic theory and practice.

Once an understanding of Lender Created Debt has been achieved many of the contradictions and much of the mumbo jumbo of traditional economic thought may be seen clearly through the lens of this powerful tool.

An excellent source on many subjects is the online encyclopedia www.wikipedia.com. For every hour spent reading this book at least twenty should be spent following the links in wikipedia and considering the ramifications of LCD on the subject. Suggested starter search terms are: economics, money, credit money, money supply, money creation, fractional reserve banking, and usury.

Chapter Ten

The Lenders Dilemma

At first it would seem that LCD lenders have it made. They benefit from an established tradition of lending practices with everyone in society trained in the habit and mechanics of borrowing and repaying loans. The money supply is kept short so there is always a market for their loans. All they have to do is sit back and collect their harvest of interest money, spend some of it, lend the rest back out.

In reality there are a lot of problems. First, to whom are the loans to be given? Someone has to be found that is knowledgeable enough to produce, but ignorant enough to pledge collateral exceeding the value of the loan in the hope of winning a rigged game.

Another is accounting. Every loan has to be continually watched; payments accounted for when made, payments demanded when late, collateral seized and sold when defaulted on. The total money in circulation has to be controlled. This requires coordination between all of the lenders that can create credit money. Growth of the parasitic secondary/sacrificial lenders has to be monitored and managed.

There is the problem of the continual collateral damage that the LCD enterprise produces in the creation of its profit. The lender poisons the society with debt and sells the cure. An analogy would be for a person to poison all of the water in the society and sell the antidote. In the act he also poisons his own water and is himself dependant on the antidote. He is

completely dependant on universal ignorance as to the cause of
this damage or he faces liabilities that far exceed his profit.

Take for example one person out of a job because steps
have been taken to lower the amount of money in circulation.

The managing lenders have deemed some control necessary
to slow the growth of secondary lenders. There are not enough
transactions available with the remaining money supply to
support sufficient production activity to include this person's
job. He develops a medical condition that would respond to
treatment if he had money to see a doctor. He doesn't have
enough money so just sits it out. His friends can't raise enough
to help him because their pay is being shorted also. Because
of the lack of attention he ends up in a coma and has to be
cared for the remaining 50 years of his life. Nothing medically
remarkable has to be done but someone has to be in attendance
at all times and someone else has to provide food shelter and
utilities. Taking this care to be worth $20.00 an hour times 24
hours in a day times 365 days a year times 50 years equals $8.76
million dollars.

This is still not a problem because lenders don't pay for
anything. The care can only be paid for by taxes on producers.
He could possibly die instead of being disabled and someone
else would have to support his family and raise his kids. An
anonymous lender somewhere in the society probably only
collected $5000.00 in interest for the elimination of that
persons job. This extreme but plausible example produces a
earning to damage ratio of lender plus1to society minus1752.

If these constantly occurring damages were properly
attributed to the lenders, it could easily be seen that the
multitude of victims have a moral right to inflict just about
whatever form and severity of retribution they could think of.
History has many examples of this exact thing happening.

To reduce the risk of this occurrence, the master lenders
allow and even encourage everyone in the society that is holding
any money, even for a short amount of time, to loan it out at
interest. In this way the trail of blame for lending is obscured
to the casual observer at the expense to the master lender of a

great portion of the interest income. In fact these secondary "Sacrificial Lenders" or SLs could possibly consume 90% or even more of the total interest income. These SLs have to be regulated by the managing/master lenders or MLs in regards to interest rates and lending practices.

As their interest income, plus the interest that the elite managing lenders are receiving is added into the final price of all goods and services in the society, inflation is intensified. The inflation is once again controlled by producing money shortage deflation, with the predictable increase in societal dependants caused by not enough money to do business with.

The master lenders now have to encourage socialist agendas to feed the dependants they have created even though socialism could potentially be very hostile to lenders who happen to be rich. The MLs have to support intrusive tax collection methods such as the income tax that require onerous reporting requirements to obtain data on source and type of income from every producer and sacrificial lender so that they may anticipate changes in money supply requirements.

The externality debt that the lenders owe to society grows with each passing day. It would be relatively easy to figure the direct costs that have been paid for by the producers. The sum of all welfare payments, food stamps, unemployment compensation, court and correctional institution cost, medicare, medicaid, social security, agricultural subsidies and about half of defense spending for the last one hundred years minus 10 percent for what would have been necessary without LCD would be a good approximation.

The indirect costs borne by society as a whole could be estimated by multiplying the direct costs by a factor of ten. These would include underpaid wages, living one's whole life and not being allowed to fully participate and contribute to society, breakup of families for financial causes, early deaths from lack of resources, and many other problems that lack of free trade have caused. $500 trillion dollars would not be an unreasonable estimate of this debt. Divided among the approximately 300 million US citizens this is a debt of 1.6 million owed to each and every person.

The current lenders having inherited the business from previous generations should rightly be considered to have inherited the liabilities. Lenders should start paying their bills or get out of the business.

The lenders have an excuse for everything and effectively shift blame that is rightfully theirs to others. It is not lenders that cause unemployment but lazy people who will not work. Lenders do not cause inflation. It is caused by greedy people charging too much. Lenders do not cause people to go to war. It is caused by nut cases with radical ideologies. Lenders do not control all of the money. It is the greedy rich people with their foot on the poor people's necks. The amazing part is how readily each of these maligned groups accepts their groups blame.

The fact is that there is not one problem of society from cancer to flea infestation that would not be improved or completely eliminated if it were not for the lenders stealing everyone's property and producing nothing in return.

The master lenders may own the society but it is a Faustian bargain and evil now rules their souls.

Chapter Eleven

The Social Contract

I will not steal your property if you will not steal mine and I will not let others steal your property if you will not let others steal mine.

Everything that is decent in a society is a direct result of its social contract. The freedom to have a place to call your home without a daily battle to the death with another person that wants it is created by social contract. The freedom to have and raise your children and not have them snatched and made into slaves, dog food or killed for sport, comes from the social contract.

Every property transfer in nature, in contrast to a social contract property exchange causes collateral damage.

Most of the property in an LCD society if not actually owned by the lenders is pledged for collateral, and property exchange is controlled by the invisible hand of the lender. This causes the ability to enter into a meaningful bilateral contract to establish social order to be greatly diminished. How can one agree to rules about property exchange when he doesn't really own any property?

Under LCD, the enumerated rights in the "Bill of Rights" all end with the unwritten suffix ", subject to the whims of the lenders."

People in the lower ranks who subsist on transfer payments rather than being paid for what they produce are fed just to pacify them. Even if they are employed, any pay rate under

$20.00 an hour could more accurately be described as a stipend than a contractual free market exchange.

To assure their ability to get a loan when needed, all members of society must perpetually patronize, praise and flatter the lenders, especially the money creating master lenders or they will be ostracized and be forced to live on the fringes of society. Lenders will not tolerate the existence of any agreements that supersede the debt that they own. This causes the abandonment of the most valuable property the society owns, the social contract.

The social contract should not be confused with a society's constitution. The social contract is more like machine code in a computer that more complicated programs are built upon. If the machine code is flawed the more complicated programs will have limitations in operation that generate contradictions in operation. Any constitution can not be interpreted without referring to the social contract in effect at the time of creation. This is dramatically illustrated by the signers of the United States Declaration of Independence. While giving speeches and eventually ratifying the document we have today containing statements such as "All men are created equal" the signer's wealth was being created by their slaves toiling without just compensation or even being recognized as human.

Never the less the writers of our constitution did a remarkable job considering the special interest groups to whom they had to cater. Interpretation of the U.S. constitution using even the basic elementary social contract as a foundation would create wonders for our society.

Chapter Twelve

Investment

Investment: "Property dedicated to a project with the expectation of creating more property in the future." In advanced social contract societies the investment of choice is the "productive investment" that uses existing property to produce new property in greater quantities and of new useful types than previously existed.

Since the word investment can mean a wide variety of things to different people it should be considered a "joker word". This is especially true if it is not made clear if it refers to a productive or nonproductive investment. If a nonproductive investment is being proposed it is essentially a natural property transaction proposition.

Agriculture projects such as the growing of crops or animal husbandry are excellent examples of productive investment. If managed properly, productive investments are capable of becoming property generators, producing more property than is invested in the particular enterprise. Productive investment is generally compatible with and compliments most advanced social contracts, yielding benefits for all in the society.

Lender Created Debt is a non-productive investment. While it can return a long term profit for the lender, if the liquidity in the society is carefully managed to control inflation, the necessary shortage of money and the included interest cost, reduces profits on all productive investments. The profits lost are far greater than the profit that the lender receives for his propagation of debt. This results in a perpetually "anemic" society that never quite works right.

With productive investment possibilities so profoundly altered in a society with active LCD, non-productive investment schemes become more attractive.

The first investment opportunity that presents itself to anyone with some free cash is of course, LCD. With the money supply being controlled by and for the benefit of the lenders, there is a ready market for anyone else that is fortunate enough to have free cash to lend. This of course maintains the luke-warm health of the society because interest payments come from and diminish honest productive profits.

The second investment that is available is that known as the "Ponzi" or pyramid scheme. This type of investment depends on an ever increasing number of new investors buying in to the particular scheme on a regular basis to buy out previous investors. Although they are non-productive, having some investors subscribing to ponzi-pyramid schemes does divert their money from the LCD market. This type of investment should be considered at best "entertainment" as whit any form of gambling, and not a prudent place to save money.

Both LCD and pyramid schemes have the seeming advantage to the prospective investor of looking simple. All that seems to be necessary is to look at promised or historical returns to understand these investments. In reality both sources of data are meaningless. Pyramid scheme data always looks great until that scheme crashes. Data collected from a ponzi operation is like a report that states; "Everything is going fine." from someone who has jumped out of a high top floor window. The favorable reports end when ground level is reached. The fact that this may take a while does not change the nature of the enterprise.

A third type of investment is predatory speculation, also known as cornering the market, attempting to hold enough of a particular type of property to control its price. There is a fine line between speculation and predatory speculation. When a certain level of speculation on any good is reached the price can be made to increase or decrease as if a planned and managed predatory scheme were in place.

The fourth type of investment is in essence natural property transfer also known as stealing. This includes criminal and unethical activity of every type known. This investment holds promise of greater profit because many citizens will not participate because of the risk.

Investment in lobbying to make certain drugs illegal yields greater profits for the drug dealers and allows politicians to steal additional tax money from producers for ineffective enforcement activity. Investing in developing skills of deception, and misrepresentation can result in getting elected to public office without the dangers of armed robbery or back alley drug deals.

The fifth and preferable type is the productive investment. The productive investment creates more valuable property, or utility, by combining, organizing and improving more common and less desirable property. Every person in the society has a better chance of prospering and also contributing to their society when productive investment is maximized.

Any particular investment today is a mix, in varying ratios, of all types of these five investments.

A large source of investment money is retirement money. Most people understand that as a result of advancing age and the frailties that result, they can not be productive forever. They realize that the day will come when their needs will exceed what they can produce. It is therefore desirable that the prudent person not consume all that he produces and to save some of this property against this inevitability.

The question is; what form should this property be in? It should be some type of property that does not lose value with time. Simply holding cash money or currency is now not an option because of the LCD caused inflation. True productive investments, such as manufacturing, distribution, service or research, usually require some expertise in the subject to know what to invest in. While some people might have the skills and background to do this, it is not suitable for the vast majority of retirement monies. The large scale speculative hoarding of non ageing commodities such as metals or land creates artificial price inflation of those commodities increasing the price paid by productive enterprises so does not benefit society.

Another large source of investment money is insurance companies. Insurance firms collect money from subscribers in accordance with their individual risk of an unforeseen misfortune, and coordinate the sharing of the cost of that individual loss among the whole group. This is an excellent stabilizing force in a society. The problem is that they must have the collected money on hand in anticipation of a claim. As described before, they cannot just hold the money because of inflation causing the money to lose buying power every day. They are now effectively forced to place that money in some sort of investment so that it holds its value. True productive investments require a different area of expertise than watching ponzi schemes grow. Also actual production is in most cases far too risky for money that is held in trust, especially with LCD ravaging the producer's profits in the society.

For retirement savings, insurance funds, and other large trust accounts, this leaves the big four non-productive investments. 1. LCD, 2. Pyramid/ponzi stock schemes, 3. Predatory speculation, 4. Financing criminal activity or a combination of all four are the primary choices.

Investment schemes such as bonds with a predictable rate of return are in reality just an investment in LCD. Most stocks are so heavily dependant on their pyramid component to ever generate a respectable dividend that they should be defined as ponzi schemes. Only in the initial public offering does any money go to the proposed production.

The real answer is to get rid of LCD so that the currency can be made stable over long periods of time and so that it can be simply held with confidence. The effect of workers getting paid what they are worth in a free market and simply holding the money until later in their lives when needed would be deflationary. Insurance and other funds simply held as currency, instead of put in play in some sort of investment scheme, would also be deflationary. This would counter other inflationary trends in the society, keeping prices accurate and low. The cost of productive enterprise investments by productive people would be lower and the individual profits greater, creating more property and well paid employment for everyone.

The idea that money has to be kept "working" is as absurd as the idea that every gun, knife, or other weapon should be kept "working" threatening someone to relinquish their property. It also has the same effect on society.

Chapter Thirteen

What About the Economists?

E conomists may be divided into two schools of thought concerning money, the credit money economists and the real money economists.

The history of the advances in understanding the world we live in by the scientific and technical disciplines is astonishingly recent. Medicine, chemistry, physics, mathematics, material science, information management, manufacturing technology and numerous others would be indecipherable to the foremost experts in each field 100 years ago, in some cases 10 years ago.

Each field is built on a succession of truths, call laws of nature that can be followed to create a predictable outcome. Sometimes it could take thousands of years for the next truth to be discovered. Sometimes a truth discovered in one discipline would facilitate understanding in another. At other times a truth that is thought to be correct and taken for granted proves false, requiring a rethinking of all theory that it was built upon.

Much of the original work in chemistry was done looking for the "philosopher's stone". This substance was claimed to be able to turn other materials into gold at the whim of the possessor. This unlimited supply of gold would make the owner master of the world.

The next best thing to the philosopher's stone was discovered by an ancient economist. The creation of gold was not as fast as could be desired, but it was relentless and got faster the longer the process worked. As you can probably guess by now the economist's "philosopher's stone" was Lender Created Debt. The debt that it creates produces gold in amounts beyond the widest imagination.

There is a type of trap used for catching monkeys in some parts of the world. It consists of a coconut that has a hole cut in it that is just large enough for a monkeys hand to go through. A piece of fruit or other treat that the monkey likes is placed inside of the coconut and the coconut is tied to a tree. When the monkey puts his hand inside of the hole in the coconut and grabs the treat his fist is too large to come back through the hole. The monkey will sit there holding his treat until someone comes and takes him away.

Lender Created Debt is the credit economist's monkey trap. It has so captivated their imagination with the promise of wealth obtained through application of compound interest that they will not let go long enough to escape. The credit economists completely ignore the fact that so many externalities are produced once simple debt becomes lender created debt that the lending transactions are negative sum. They will not admit that the economic model that is used to justify LCD does not produce prices that reflect reality. They also ignore the issue of scale. If a certain amount of lending is beneficial to a society where does that benefit end? When the lending amounts to one quarter of the money supply? When the lending is five times the money supply? When the lending is one hundred times the money supply? The credit economists even have a tool called marginal utility theory that could shine the light of reality on LCD, but dare not apply it to interest and lending because it would be heresy to the lenders.

This means that all theories that rely on the credit economist's models can not produce reliable or accurate predictions of reality. Any chemist, physicist or engineer would be embarrassed if he couldn't describe an accurate way to measure a pound or kilogram. The credit economists will just say a dollar is worth what it is worth and advise you to not ask too many questions or capital will not get allocated properly.

Another quirk of the credit economist is the aloofness they practice in their economy fantasy model. They purport to be exempt and above any ethical considerations. Any chemist that routinely poisoned his customers, any electrician who wired a house in such a way that when the owner turned on a light it caused the next door neighbor to be electrocuted or any engineer who let a nuclear plant radiate millions of people would probably have some regret and take some steps not to let it happen again.

Not the credit economist. He looks at reports of credit money dealings every day yet sees no problem with some people not being able to work, others not being able to participate in society, the lenders getting richer, the poor getting poorer and every child being born $160,000 in debt and does not even wonder what the cause is.

The credit economist's definition of "the free market" includes the activities of the master lenders and the sacrificial lenders stealing property through LCD, without themselves producing anything of value.

Consider an electrical generating company that consumes fuel to spin generators to produce electricity. Their business model would require users of that electricity to pay based on how much of that electricity each one uses. To measure that electricity, a kilowatt hour meter is installed in the wire between the power plant and each users load. A technician, who installs and calibrates the kWh meters, adjusts every meter except his own to register more electricity than is actually flowing through it. He adjusts his meter to run backwards as if he were producing the electricity that he uses at his house. Since he has cohorts at the electric company he is sent a check for the electricity that he supposedly produces. Other people find out about the scheme and threaten to expose him if he doesn't adjust their meters so that they get a check also. Eventually, half of the electricity used is not being paid for by the correct user and some are paying double what the electricity is worth. The management at the electric company finds out and keeps quiet because of their potential liability. Each day they take any steps necessary to keep the problem secret, devoting all resources of the company to the project.

Not every one can afford to pay double for the electricity that they use. They have their meters turned off and live in the dark. This increases the remaining honest payer's bill to three times what the electricity they use is worth.

The suppliers of the fuel happen to be honest payers but since the cost of electricity that they must use to dig up and grind the coal to produce that fuel has gone up, they must increase the cost of the fuel to cover the increased electricity cost of producing it.

This cause and effect scenario could go on practically forever. As a result of inaccurate measurement the business model is worthless because no one knows what electricity costs. This is what the economists are letting happen to their discipline by not admitting that included interest and transactional exclusion invalidates their standard of measure, the dollar or whatever monetary unit it may be.

This is not an exact analogy because the electric meter is purposely made to read incorrectly for private benefit. The electrical engineers undoubtedly have standards and a measurement discipline or they couldn't get the generators and other electrical devices to work properly. The credit economists are letting their standard be tampered with by not taking into account the interest cost and the restriction of the money supply that is necessary to keep cost from being passed back to the lender.

Interest is theoretically supposed to measure the "time value" of money but money has no value in and of itself. The time value resides in the product or property that has already been created by some producer. This value is usurped and stolen from the producer by the lender, especially the money creating lender. Money has no value unless there is something to buy.

The quantity of money in a system can be calibrated to save the lenders from their own inflation or to reflect the value of property in an economy; it can not do both at the same time.

At the meter technician's house where electricity is supposedly created from nothing, the definition and value of an amp, volt, watt or second would have to be changed for his meter to be judged accurate.

There is simply no way to have it both ways.

Unfortunately the LCD monkey trap seems to efficiently capture and create a credit money economist out of every economist that is exposed to it. It is as if a sinister Dr. Jekyll and Mr. Hyde potion had transformed every chemist into some kind of beast. There are seemingly no real economists at this time that know how real money works.

All major disciplines have some ancient roots in religious fervor but have eventually progressed to the point of being scientific. The field of mechanical design still has some devotees to the perfection of a perpetual motion machine. One basic scheme would be to connect the shaft of an electric motor to turn the shaft of an electrical generator. The wires from the generator are then connected to the motor. Their theory says that all that is now necessary is to give the shaft a spin and the machine will run forever.

Truly irrationally exuberant perpetual motion devotees would also believe this system would create free excess electricity to run all manner of useful electrical devices. In fact, less energy is produced than consumed and the machine comes to a halt when the energy of the initial spin is exhausted. This level of advancement is where the credit economists are at present. This is made quite evident by their convincing of the federal government to give the U.S. economy a spin with trillions of dollars more debt. The credit economists are convinced that a big enough spin, at exactly the right time, will show the world the unlimited scope of their unappreciated genius.

The field of credit economics has turned into an anachronism in the ever growing group of true scientific disciplines because it has actively avoided, in devoted deference to the lenders, studying the properties of real money. The field of credit economics remains a faith based religion that includes human sacrifice as part of its rites. It keeps a morbid score of these sacrifices by computing unemployment, and poverty level figures among others. They can preach all day but they preach of faith not reality.

It is greatly hoped that some truly exceptional economists will consider LCD now that it is described and begin to reform their chosen discipline. Better late than never!

If the credit economists can not get their scholarly act together, we will have to depend on the engineering disciplines of other fields to straighten out the money. Any competent electrical, mechanical, chemical or scientific design team could develop an accurate model, establish system requirements, calibration protocol, quality control procedures and project implementation timelines like they do everyday in the course of a days work on systems far more complicated than monetary score keeping systems.

Chapter Fourteen

Government

Representative government is rendered impotent for the same reasons that the social contract is ignored. Although styled as a republic with democratically elected representatives to manage the government, the underlying truth is that no one truly owns and controls any property in the United States of America except the managing lenders.

People are allowed to believe that they can own property but they are effectively sharecroppers on the lenders property. They are usually left alone as long as they produce. They are even allowed to keep a little of their own production to give them false hope. The theoretical ownership is a management "carrot" that allows the producers to believe that they are producing for themselves so they work harder than slaves would.

Decisions that involve lender's interests are always decided in their favor. No one, not even the elected representatives can afford to piss off the lenders. All daily decisions are left to the sharecroppers/peons/producers.

When any government, federal, state or local actually tries to honestly collect reasonable taxes and manage the public goods such as roads, public defense, law enforcement and others it is also affected by the included interest and shortage of money problems. Since an ever increasing fraction of any price in Lender Created Debt consists of interest, reduced production capacity, externality control and dependant support the government itself is constantly short of money.

The ability to tax itself solvent is counteracted by the population's resistance to increased taxes because everyone is a victim of the LCD. It is necessary for the government to borrow its share of the Lender Created Debt to help keep some money in circulation. Once this avenue is maxed out, use of the coercive power of government to correct the monetary shortfall creates a government that can not be trusted. The government's shortfall is addressed with a million different fees and fines. Everyday more of the government's time is consumed in the creating, management and adjusting of these fines and fees. This amounts to stealing of property directly from individuals with the feeble excuse that the guilty should pay for their own rehabilitation. Activities are made illegal not in the public's interest but to generate revenue from fees, fines and contributions for special interest groups.

One example would be access to premises. Say you allowed workmen to come into your house to perform some repairs or improvements. It would be bad business to underpay them and let them steal whatever they wanted to compensate themselves for the shortfall. Government requires certain liberties to carry out their duties, just as the workmen need the liberty to come into the house. This should not be construed as a right to steal property that they are entrusted to protect.

There are always some people in a society that will not abide by a social contract and through inappropriate behavior steal or destroy other people's property. All society benefits from this antisocial behavior being controlled. The government's proper job in supporting the social contract is to evaluate these misfits and re-educate or take them out of society if necessary.

Soliciting bribes in the form of fines, fees and court costs as a part of this evaluation is antisocial. The government, federal, state and local should be an example of all of the best principles that create a society. No matter how technically complicated the bribe oversight process is, the fundamentals do not work. Antisocial conduct can not be controlled by people devoted to the concept that stealing is good. It does not matter that one person makes the law, another assesses it, another collects it and yet another spends it. It is all theft and thieves, even thieves with a really complicated bureaucracy can not be trusted any more than hungry wolves can be trusted by sheep.

No government should take any person's property without full compensation, except as their fair share of tax to pay for public goods. Property should never have to be given up to obtain the government's favor or secure one's own rights.

A simple example would be seatbelts. Government should have earned enough respect that all that should be necessary would be to tell drivers that it has been discovered that seatbelts save lives and suggest that drivers and passengers use them. As it is now, no one can be sure if the suggestion originates from enforcement jurisdictions looking for other sources of revenue, manufactures that sell seatbelts who have paid off congress, megalomaniacal legislators or some combination of all of these.

Once government is allowed to believe they have been delegated the power to steal, nothing anyone in government says or does can be taken at face value. Having once sold their virtue they will engage in any criminal activity. Everyone knows what they have become and all that needs to be negotiated is price.

No parties to a workable social contract can delegate the power to steal to a government because they have exchanged the right to take others property for the right to have their own property secure.

The master lenders do have the authority to tell government to steal because they own all of the property. They support stealing to help pay for government expenditures because higher taxes compete with interest payments. Government stealing is also promoted by the lenders to provide food and basic necessities for dependants so they don't get desperate enough to fight.

It must also be kept in mind that the state and local governments are simply doing their best to play the LCD game that has been forced upon them like all of the other producers in society.

Chapter Fifteen

Our Present Situation

2,000 years after Jesus threw the moneychangers out of the temple, here we are in the 21st century stilled plagued by debt. At this time the USA is at least $50,000,000,000,000 in debt. This amounts to over $160,000 for every person in the USA. Each birth certificate issued is collateral against the debt and evidence of a lien on the productive capability of that infant. Some manage to pay it. Most do not.

Just to pay 6% interest on this debt each person owes $26.00 per day or $9600.00 per 365 day year. A reasonable estimate of $20.00 in externality damage is probably caused for each $1.00 in interest paid so the individual debtor's actual loss is $520.00 of stolen value every day.

Actually paying this debt is impossible, not because of its magnitude, but because of the underlying LCD that creates it. What has to be understood is that it is never meant to be paid off. It exists to calculate interest payments from.

The lenders of society live off of this debt. They collect interest money every day and do not contribute any production to society in exchange for it, just externalities. They do not pay for the externalities that they create. Earlier in this book these accumulated externalities, which the lenders should rightfully pay, were estimated presently at $500 trillion dollars. Ten times the total debt owed.

Because of this debt our money does not work. Some people are overpaid, some people are underpaid and many can not get paid at all.

Because the money does not work, our society has split
into three basic types of people.

1. Producers that do the work and create property. Most of
the value of their production is stolen from them through the
Lender Created Debt trap.

2. Lenders who utilize the LCD trap and are parasites on
society.

3. Dependants, whose ranks are increased several fold
above natural levels as a result of the LCD trap stealing not only
any property than they produce faster than they can produce it,
but also their tools of production.

Memberships in these groups overlap with some people
being a member of all three.

Parasites in nature are usually one organism that feeds
off of another, taking advantage of some weakness in their
defense. In the human society LCD facilitates the capability of
metamorphosis between the three states of parasite, dependant
and producer. This can occur many times in a person's life as
their fortunes change. If the producer's productivity increases
they use their earnings to become lenders. If the lender
population grows faster than production, some of them start
to get hungry and have to become producers again. If they fail a
metamorphosis they end up as a dependant.

This produces exactly what we see today, a weak, mean,
unjust society with a lot of dependants, demonstrating a classic
example of parasitic equilibrium.

Here we are, a society that has walked on the moon, with
new discoveries and technology being created at an exponential
rate, a nation of peons, allowing a group of self serving lenders
to prey on society to the exclusion of many fellow citizens.

Notwithstanding all of these modern day miracles we
readily accept real compensation that is diminished by as much
as 90% or completely forfeited by many, in exchange for the
ability to borrow money.

Are we going to pass this situation on to the next generation
or do something about it?

Can any society exist without the guidance of the invisible
hand of the lenders?

Chapter Sixteen

Aspects of a Cure, the "Dulin Plan"

A cure would have to address multiple subjects. Elimination of the debt, putting a trustworthy currency in circulation, compensation for dependants so they could try to rebuild what is left of their lives and reaffirming the social contract that is the basis for our society.

The LCD lenders can not begin to compensate the producers and dependants for all the property they have taken from them and never hope to pay the dependants for all of the opportunities in life of which they have been deprived. The lenders are parasites by training, occupation and inclination. Their only true asset is the debt chain around each producer's neck that the lender jerks when he wants something done. The best that can be hoped from them is cooperation to end the legacy of LCD practice as quickly and efficiently as possible, so everyone can get back to living their own productive life.

We have in the United States of America, a well established system of non-violently addressing the grievances of the society thru the representative government. Unless representation is demand by the producers, the lenders interests will be represented first for all of the favors that they can bestow and have bestowed in the past.

Since this is a problem with a public good, the money, and since the federal government not the states has the constitutional duty to create and maintain a money supply we should work through our elected federal representatives and senators to effect a workable cure. This might take a while if the members of congress do not take this duty seriously and they have to be voted out.

There is no exaggeration in stating that money management is the primary job of the Federal Government. It comes even before national security because defense is compromised without maximum production capability in place. If our countries monetary dealings with its own people and other countries are honest, and without the hidden agenda and preferential treatment of the lenders, the chance of war is greatly diminished. In allowing its monetary responsibilities to be assumed by the lenders, the federal government has actually created most of the problems such as poverty, most wars and insecurity of the nation that it purports to be so busy addressing.

Maximum efficiency and accuracy of property exchange for the convenience of all citizens, is the most important public good for the government to supply and manage.

If the decision is made to correct this money problem the first actions would be the individual's responsibility.

1. Talk to friends, neighbors and colleagues so that they understand the problem. Give them this book. Always keep in mind that this is a public problem and requires a public solution.

2. Communicate with government representatives to let them know what is required of them. Let them know that there is a new understanding of how money and debt works. Identify any representative that puts lenders interests ahead of their other constituents and vote them out of office.

Remember that your representatives are not your keepers or your Gods, but are workmen with a job to do. They are put into office not to rule you but to represent you and your property. If you let them conspire with lenders to harm others in society you are the responsible one. Remind them of the nature of this relationship every time you communicate.

Nothing deserves more respect than any workman from

any social strata conscientiously performing their duties. Also nothing is more contemptible than a workman given liberties and trust to perform a task utilizing these for his own gain.

If you are a producer and want to be paid full value for your production let your representative know.

If you are a dependant and want compensation for the circumstances the lenders have forced on you let your representative know.

If you are a lender and want them to assist you in stealing other people's property you probably already have their phone number so let your representatives know. An elected official is not supposed to represent criminal cartel enterprise but it has worked up until now.

3. Get your own property in order. If you have investments, review all of them to make sure that they are not LCD, ponzi, hording or criminal in nature. Productive investments will always remain valuable, especially if the LCD can be brought under control.

4. Do not default on loans or other obligations. Pay every bill and every debt that you have agreed to. It can now be understood that these obligations are the result of duress, but a civilized response is called for. This is a societal problem and must be addressed by societal action.

The property rights of all three groups concerned have to be taken into account.

Producers make and pay for everything. They will be the ones paying for the restoration of our democratic republic. Let them get to work.

Many dependants will become producers as soon as there is enough money to keep score of trade and remedial education opportunities for them to learn. Make education available. This step is vitally important because leaving a vacuum of unemployed idle citizens negates many benefits of this cure.

All lenders presently earn their living through parasitism. They owe debts to society that they can never repay. They need to be reeducated to be producers. Stop the parasitism and provide them educational opportunities.

The first impulse would be to declare all debts extinguished but this would unnecessarily hurt the sacrificial "shield" lenders that the master lenders have allowed to proliferate. The great majority of the sacrificial lenders diligently strive to be decent members of society. They are hostages to the master lenders and have no idea of the damage that they are causing others.

There is no actual real money in circulation since all real money has long been replaced with credit money. Many people's savings are in the form of interest bearing debt. Accrual of interest has to be stopped on all debt so that its repayment can begin. This will immediately reduce the externalities that generate most of the waste.

The principle of every outstanding debt should be paid but with no further accrual of interest allowed, insuring the integrity of retirement funds and other savings. We need a soft landing not a crash.

If understood by the sacrificial lenders, this should be seen as greatly preferable to the "decimation" by inflation or deflation, as practiced by the master lenders. It is important that every person retain the greatest portion of their savings.

The next actions would be performed by the Federal government.

1. Write and ratify a social contract so that a common understanding may exist among all members of our society of everyone's most basic rights and responsibilities. No more "making it up as you go" for all branches of government.

2. Fix a starting date. Put a tax on interest accrued for any reason by the lender or creditor after this date, of 200% per year to be computed and paid by the lender quarterly whether the interest is collected or not. If debt is accruing by any mechanism whether collected or not, the tax must be paid. Correct the definition of interest to include any increase in debt as a result of time. Keep this tax in effect until the total debt is less than 5% of the total real money supply. The purpose of this tax is to give an incentive to lenders or other creditors to forgive the interest portion of the debt making the total debt payable. Tax may not be passed on to debtor.

3. Require that every debt, every lien and other evidence of debt that is outstanding be registered and interest tax paid to the Internal Revenue Service within three months. Registration would include a registration tax of 2% of debt balance payable by the lender, not to be passed on to the debtor, on the total value of the debt with annual renewal and 2% of balance annual renewal fee payable quarterly.

Registration information, supplied by the lender/holder of debt, would include total sum and term to retire the debt including interest amount if not forgiven, repayment schedule, lender name, debtor name, date of initiation, contact information and any other useful information.

If notice of completed registration is not sent to debtor within 30days of registration the debt is to be considered paid in full.

The purpose of this registration is to accurately keep track of total debt in the society and begin to pay for educational opportunities for producers, dependants and lenders alike to put the centuries of deprivation behind us. Also as an incentive to retire relic debt that formed as a result of the centuries of LCD.

4. Began putting non-debt real money into circulation. As the credit money disappears it will need to be replaced with a real money supply that is issued for the convenience of the public and not some favored group. Assume that a real money supply engineering design study suggested that 10 trillion dollars would need to be put into circulation over the next five years. Taking into account a population of 300 million people this would require that every person with a social security number would receive $555.55 every month for five years. This could be calibrated as needed to counteract inflation or deflation.

The most convenient way to do this would be with a debit card account system like is done now with food assistance. The key is that every citizen gets the same amount interest free. The goal of the Federal government would be that the value of the money is to be maintained with no inflation or deflation. This is a great convenience for everyone in society and our money would be trustworthy in the rest of the world.

5. Reform the tax system. Cancel every present federal state and local tax except for the interest and debt tax. Cancel all unpaid existing tax liabilities or regulatory liabilities as relics of the LCD that created and maintained them. Replace them with a 2% transaction tax on change in ownership of money. Every time a dollar is spent 2%, 1% from the buyer and 1% from the seller goes to the treasury. Every time a check is written 2% goes to the treasury. Currency transactions between individuals over $100.00 would be subject to the 2% tax.

Since there would be many points of sale, the collection should be managed by the states just like sales tax is now. The local, state, and federal governments would then devise a formula to divide the proceeds for each to use for their own purposes.

For sales across city, county, state lines or out of country it would be equitable for both the buyers and seller's jurisdictions to split credit for the transaction 50-50. If both jurisdictions are outside of the country the exchange would only be subject to a small fee of perhaps .5% to pay for cost of the money system.

This solves the problem of internet sales and of low cost goods subsidized by what is essentially slave labor in foreign countries. Tax on commerce would effectively be applied directly to commerce and not unfairly to businesses in one country. Friendly countries could instantly use actual debt free real dollars.

The tax rate could only be changed by 2/3 majority popular vote.

Federal, State and Local governmental entities should save at least 20% of their income for emergencies and large capital purchases. They will immediately be in better financial condition because of the elimination of the interest portion of their debt. There will be no borrowing or loaning with interest by governmental entities.

Government at all levels would cease the taking of property in the form of fines, fees, penalties and levies. They should work to manage the tax money have they have allotted for the maximum public benefit and never be allowed to supplement their income with misuse of their authority. This would be a step in creating a trustworthy government at all levels. Government at all levels should get back to work providing public goods as is their mandate. Education and health care both need immediate consideration.

6. In addition to committing to a stable dollar value with no inflation or deflation, the federal government should establish inflation free savings accounts for retirement, medical, insurance and other deposits. They would not draw interest, be invested, borrowed from or be subject to any tricky financial manipulations, but would be compensated for inflation out of the federal government's savings account. The savings accounts and all depository accounts would require physical proof of every dollar deposited by actually holding currency that is certified by a numbering system. Depositories would be subject to regular audits by all levels of government.

Epilogue

This is the conclusion of my personal opinion of how money works, how sometimes it does not work and how it can be fixed.

Your opinions, comments and suggestions are welcome and appreciated. Please visit. www.lendercreateddebt.com

Glossary

Calibration of money — Increasing or decreasing of the quantity of money in circulation in an economy to regulate prices.

Capital — joker word/money/ property/ tools/assets/debt/ means of production

Credit Economist — Person who specializes in understanding property exchanges in societies that have credit money as the circulating currency. Characterized by use of "joker words" to reconcile unworkable theories.

Credit Money — Money that comes into existence as an interest bearing loan. When the loan is paid the money ceases to exist but the unpaid interest created debt remains in circulation in society. Due to the unlimited issuance possibilities and the inflation created by the interest debt being incorporated into prices, credit money is calibrated to minimize inflation.

Democracy — Societal system where political authority derives from decisions made by a majority of citizens in that system. Any decision or course of action is theoretically possible, from executing the minority and taking their property to declaring laws of nature invalid, as long as the majority concurs.

Externality — Collateral damage/ unintended consequences/ secondary consequences/ secondary damage

Free Market — joker word/unencumbered trade of property at a price determined by market conditions/ manipulation of financial tricks to obtain property that would be considered fraud or stealing if it did not involve interest or debt.

Haveto — Circumstance that requires a relinquishment of property.

Interest—Any creation or increase in debt as a function of time. This would include late payment penalties and any fee or fine resulting as a function of a time based occurrence on a debt.

Investment—joker word/ can mean nonproductive as well as productive investment or any combination of the two.

Joker Word—word that is poorly defined allowing its meaning to be misconstrued as necessary to fit the occasion.

Lender Created Debt—Debt of such a magnitude in relation to the money supply that it can not be repaid unless the lender/lenders spend all of the interest earnings from the instant it began accruing.

LCD—An acronym for "Lender Created Debt".

Lender—Person who lets other person or persons use property, especially money in exchange for payment of interest.

Master Lender—Lender who controls the creation of credit money.

ML—Acronym for "Master Lender"

Money—Token agreed upon by a society to represent value used to valuate and keep score of property exchanges.

Natural Property Transfer—The way property is transferred in nature without any regard for ownership, compensation or other party's damage from the transfer. / theft.

NPT—Acronym for "Natural Property Transfer"

Peon—A person held in compulsory servitude to a master for the working out of indebtedness.

Productive Investment—Property employed and managed to create new property. Specifically excludes schemes that create haveto circumstances causing transfer of vulnerable people's property.

Real Economist—Person who specializes in understanding property transactions occurring in societies that have real money as the circulating currency.

Real Money—Money that accurately models real property value and transactions in a real economy. Money that is free of special interest group control and therefore is capable of being managed and calibrated for maximum efficiency of property exchange and universal access.

Republic—joker word/ System of government that recognizes and provides the individual's basic right to property and the freedoms necessary to exercise that right as long as other's rights are not infringed. / Word used by despots to camouflage and confuse activities.

Secondary Lenders—"sacrificial lender" / "expendable lender"/ " shield lender" One who lends their own money at the pleasure and tolerance of the "Master Lender/s" Called sacrificial because due to higher public visibility and being more numerous they bear the first onslaught of public wrath for the general public's discovering that their property is being appropriated by lenders. By bearing the initial attack and giving the "Master Lender/s" time to hide they provide a formidable defense. They can also be bankrupted at the whim of the "master lender/s" to adjust the ratio of lenders to borrowers in the society.

SLs—An acronym for "Sacrificial Lenders"/ "Secondary Lenders"

Slavery—Theory of ownership of a person as property that includes the ownership of anything they produce. Slave's cooperation and production usually maximized by threat of physical harm.

Social Contract—Most basic understanding of each individual in society of his rights/benefits and responsibilities to other individuals that has been agreed to and formalized as law so that it may be legally enforced.

Socialism—System of government where ownership of all property, with no distinction between public and private, is vested in the government. All property exchanges hands thru government decree instead of bidding process. Due to absence of token money socialism is immune to LCD. Partial socialism often proposed as solution for manifest problems in LCD infected society.

Transactional Exclusion—Denial of some members of society the ability to participate in efficient property transfer caused by a shortage of money. Can range from being underpaid for property, especially labor, to not being able to be paid for property at all.

Note on word meanings. When communicating with anyone, credit economist or lay person it is important not to accept their use of joker words such as "capital", "investment", "free market" and many others. Communication of ideas requires work on the part of both parties. It is the responsibility of the speaker to accurately and truthfully explain in language that is understood and not just baffle the listener with bull or insider jargon to make them feel inferior. If you do not understand, ask for clarification. The listener has the responsibility of considering what is being said and honestly comparing it to reality.